ry editorship of J. Jeffery Auer

Interracial Communication

Under the advi

Interracial
Communication
Andrea L. Rich
University of California, Los Angeles

HARPER & ROW, PUBLISHERS
New York   Evanston   San Francisco   London

**To
John**

Sponsoring Editor: Voras D. Meeks
Project Editor: Robert Ginsberg
Production Supervisor: Stefania J. Taflinska

Interracial Communication

Library of Congress Cataloging in Publication Data
Rich, Andrea L
   Interracial communication.

   1. United States—Race question.
2. Intercultural communication. I. Title.
E185.615.R52   301.45′1042′0973   73–9810
ISBN 0–06–045391–5

Contents

Preface

It has been almost two decades now since Rosa Parks, weary from a day's work, defied generations of social convention and refused to move to the back of the bus. To some, this was the beginning of the modern black revolution; to others, such a revolution had existed in various forms from the very beginning of American slavery. Rosa Park's action was nationally significant on both a personal and a symbolic level. As an individual she said "No!" to an institution long revered in her geographical region. As a symbol she represented the beginning of the move to overturn a series of role relationships, and that movement eventually extended far beyond blacks and whites to include most of the ethnic groups who regard themselves as oppressed by whites.

The revolution of various racial and ethnic groups in our country has brought with it a series of opposing philosophies regarding the appropriate relationship between the races. Ironically the tension of the times has so polarized various groups that certain militant blacks and conservative whites find themselves agreeing, for different reasons, of course, that mixing between whites and blacks should be taboo. The integrationists of the 1950s and early 1960s, those whites and blacks who rode the freedom buses together, have become objects of scorn in some radical circles. The term "integration" has come to be viewed by young ethnic-group members as a euphemism for "watering down" the racial and ethnic culture, another form of white colonialism.

At the same time, pressure to open predominantly white institutions to nonwhites has resulted in changes in the composition of universities and colleges throughout the country. Where previously only the elite of racial and ethnic groups were admitted to the tertiary level of education, government-sponsored, high-potential programs now recruit promising nonwhite students regardless of past performance and qualifications. This new influx of students has made new demands on old institutions. "It is not enough," say the new recruits, "to be given a higher education; it must be a relevant education, an education that deals with our unique problems, an education that is aware of the part we and our people have played in this country, an education that will affect our ability to maintain our identity and to serve the future of our communities." Thus, through pressure, programs of "ethnic studies" are born across the nation. The goals of such programs are frequently defined only in general terms, but most agree that an ethnic orientation must be maintained, that new models must be found for appropriate behavior and values to replace the previous all-white models. The "ethnic studies" approach is not segregationist, nor is it integrationist; rather it is aimed at the establishment and preservation of a full ethnic identity that can remain independent from, and impervious to, the colonial tendencies of the larger white power structure.

Despite this desire for autonomy and independence from white control, various degrees of interracial and interethnic interaction are an obvious necessity where complete social, economic, and political separation do not exist. It is to facilitate such necessary interracial communication that this book is dedicated, and its emphasis is on the inevitability of—the practical necessity for—such interaction.

The racial and ethnic revolutions have made interracial communication increasingly tense and hostile. Part of this may be attributed to the change in role behavior and role expectation of the participants. Old rituals in interaction between white and non-white are no longer appropriate, for individuals refuse to behave in a manner consistent with their previously defined and projected stereotype. The "rules of the game" are constantly changing; hence interracial and interethnic communicators have little or no information on which to base their own behavior and to predict responses from other communicators.

This study attempts to explain the dynamics of interracial communication. It offers descriptions of various interracial interaction situations and possible reasons for the existence of problems in interracial communication. It does not offer prescriptions for "good" interracial communication; such value judgments have merit only if they are viewed within the context of the purpose of the individual interaction. If the goal of interracial interaction participants is to express hostility toward each other, then the interaction is "good" if it is provoking and angry. If the goal, however, is to solve problems jointly, then high degrees of animosity may prove to be an interference.

The book, therefore, is not a philosophical treatise in favor of integration or segregation. It does not assert that interracial communication is "good" or "bad." It recognizes only that interracial communication exists in various forms and will continue to exist unless radical changes in the structure of our society occur. It is a book for those who are engaged in communication among races, whether in the school, in the social sphere, or in the working community. It is designed not to tell communicators how to behave in such situations but rather to introduce them to the factors influencing them in interracial and interethnic interaction.

It is hoped that teachers on every educational level will find this book helpful in adjusting to the many problems that interracial situations pose for contemporary educators. The final chapter, "An Approach to Teaching Interracial Communication," presents a plan for teaching a course such as the one for which this book was designed. That chapter, together with the activities and suggestions at the ends of the other chapters of the book, should provide the teacher as well as the student with a concrete foundation for conducting productive interracial communication exercises.

Many thanks are due my research assistants Winifred Allen, Jr., Gale Schroeder, and Beverly Merrill. I am especially indebted to Dennis Ogawa for sharing his insights with me. And I must extend my deepest thanks to my husband and children for their patience and endurance.

Andrea L. Rich

Interracial Communication

And herein lies the tragedy of the age; not that men
are poor, all men know something of poverty; not that
men are wicked, who is good? Not that men are ignorant,
what is Truth? Nay, but that men know so little of men.

W. E. B. DuBois

Introduction to Interracial Communication

DEFINITION OF COMMUNICATION

Definitional Problem

During the past two decades, the study of "communication" has become increasingly more far-reaching in scope. From areas as disparate as engineering and theater arts, communication theories have developed. Sociologists, social psychologists, anthropologists, psychologists, linguists, speech researchers, and other specialists have turned to the study of communication in an attempt to understand human behavior. Each discipline has defined the term "communication" differently in keeping with the emphasis and background of the individual researchers. Barnlund delineates the increasing complexity in reaching consensus on the meaning of "communication":

Communication has been conceived structurally (sender-message-receiver), functionally (encoding-decoding), and in terms of intent (expressive-instrumental). It has been defined with reference to source (production of messages), channel (signal transmission), receiver (attribution of meaning), code (symbolizing), effect (evoking of response), and in ways that combine several of these criteria. To some, communication is "the process of transmitting stimuli" (Schramm), "the establishment of a commonage" (Morris), "conveying meaning" (Newcomb), or "all the procedures by which one mind affects another" (Weaver). To others, it is "interaction by means of signs and symbols" (Lundberg), "the sharing of activity, excitement, information" (Hefferline), or "the signals that individuals make to each other or which they detect in each other and which may be conscious or unconscious" (Cameron). Nearly every communicative element, function, or effect has been made the focus of some definition at some time.[1]

It is not the purpose of this book to explore the merits of the various approaches to the study and definition of communication. Rather we intend to arrive at a functional definition of communication relevant to the nature of the interaction that occurs in interracial and interethnic settings.

Homeostatic Theory

Communicative behavior, like other forms of human behavior, can be studied from a homeostatic point of view. "Homeostasis" is merely another word for "balance," man's need to maintain a state of physiological, psychological, and social harmony. Much human motivation can be attributed to the drive to remain in a balanced state. When man is hungry, his physiological state is one of imbalance; his body has a need, and he is therefore motivated to act to satisfy his need. Once he has procured and digested food, he restores balance to his body. Hunger, for the time being, ceases to be a motivating factor in his behavior. He then may realize that he is thirsty or tired and will set into motion a series of behavioral patterns designed to restore his body again to a homeostatic condition. When man is cold, he shivers to restore warmth to his body; when he is hot, he perspires to cool himself.

Frequently the ability for man to maintain a state of homeostasis rests with the capacity and willingness of others to satisfy his needs. A baby is hungry, but he cannot supply himself with food; he must in some manner reveal his state of need to another. He is thus supplied with the motivation to "communicate." The following apocryphal story reveals the relationship between communication and homeostasis:

There was once born into a family a boy who never spoke. When he was very young, his parents took him to a series of specialists to determine the cause of the problem, but none were able to cure the boy. When he reached the age of fifteen years and had never uttered a word, his parents finally came to accept the permanence of the boy's affliction. One evening, while the family was seated at the dinner table, the boy looked up and said: "Please pass the ketchup." Astonished and delighted, the father said: "But, my boy, you have never spoken, and suddenly you show us that you can speak. Why have you never spoken before?" The boy replied: "Everything was all right up to now."

People communicate because they must interact with their environment in order to satisfy their needs. The ideal result of the most perfect communication would be silence; all needs would have been satisfied, and the individual would exist in a perfect state of balance, not motivated to interact further in search of homeostasis.

Communication Models

In an attempt to delineate clearly the properties of the process of communication, researchers have turned increasingly to the presentation of models. According to Barnlund, "A theory or a model is an attempt to represent in symbolic form the underlying relations alleged to exist among the objects or forces that make up a particular event or system."[2] Such a model aids in structuring events and in clarifying the existing structure of those events. Effective models should aid in developing new ways of approaching the phenomenon they represent and identify variables for further study.[3]

Although models aid us in structuring our thoughts regarding certain phenomena, they may also mislead us either by oversimplifying a complex phenomenon or by overelaborating simple events. In either case, destructive distortion may result. The most important pitfall to avoid when offering a model is to regard the model as an end in itself. The primary function of a model is to aid the researcher in translating its component parts into explicit testable hypotheses.[4]

Typical of the communication models developed in communication research is that of Berlo:[5]

source	message	channel	receiver
communication skills	content	seeing	communication skills
attitudes	code	hearing	attitudes
knowledge	treatment	touching	knowledge
social system		smelling	social system
culture		tasting	culture

In this case the source, governed by his various attributes and driven by his need to communicate, encodes a message that is transmitted through a channel to a receiver, who decodes and responds based on his unique attributes. Many similar models exist,[6] with modifications based on variations in the handling of noise and feedback, but in general most models include four significant variables: (1) the source of the communication, or the communicator, (2) the receiver or interpreter, (3) the content, and (4) the situation in which the communication occurs.

For purposes of the theoretical model of intercultural and interracial communication, we shall view communication as a process whereby a source elicits a response in a receiver through the transmission of a message, be it sign or symbol, verbal or nonverbal. It is necessary to include nonverbal and sign behavior in our definition of communication because intercultural communication frequently occurs without the benefit of a symbolic system that is shared by the communicators.

A MODEL OF INTERCULTURAL AND INTERRACIAL COMMUNICATION

International Communication

K. S. Sitaram suggests that "international communication" is communication between political structures, rather than between cultures or individuals.[7] It is communication conducted between nations, frequently carried on by representatives of those nations. The communicators are either national leaders or their envoys. In the latter case, a government representative seldom has the power to allow himself to be persuaded to any view other than that which represents his government's policy. This, in effect, explains much of the communication failure in the United Nations. Here speakers address more than just the immediate audience of international representatives; they use the speaking platform to project national images and propaganda to the world. Members of the immediate audience are not at liberty to be persuaded, for they, too, must hold the diplomatic line of their countries.

The language of diplomacy falls within the domain of international communication. Here ambiguity rather than specificity is valued in order to allow nations to rationalize their deeds more easily in accordance with stated government policy. Euphemisms such as "premature antifascist" (communist) and "preventive reaction strike" (offensive attack) sprinkle the lexicon of international communication.

International communication as observed in the Paris peace talks, Radio Free Europe, and United Nations debates is far removed from our concept of individual human interaction. We define it here merely to distinguish it from the primary concern of this chapter: the development of a structure describing intercultural and interracial communication.

Intercultural Communication

"Culture is the sum total of the learned behaviors of a group of people which are generally considered to be the tradition of that people and are transmitted from generation to generation."[8] By "intercultural communication" we mean communication between *peoples* of different cultures. The important distinction here between intercultural communication and international communication is that individuals, not representatives of nations, are communicating. Model I represents a graphic presentation of our concept of intercultural communication. A and B represent two communicating cultures. (A_1 and B_1 would represent the interacting individuals within those cultures.) The important assumption here is that these cultures do not and have not historically existed in a colonial relationship in which one of the cultures has dominated the other for any long period of time. (Hence the circles do not overlap.) This communication occurs between peoples, perhaps, though not necessarily, within a diadic structure.

Model I

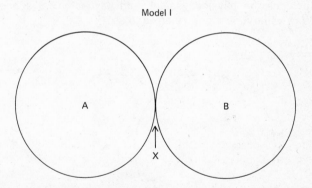

The communicators may or may not share a symbolic system. In the case of an American speaking with an Australian, intercultural communication occurs within relatively the same symbolic framework. In this case, the X of the model would refer to that shared system (the English language). In the case of a Frenchman attempting to communicate with a German, a common symbolic system may not be shared; the communicators will thus invent an on-the-spot system or resort to representational structures such as pictures, primitive sign language, or any type of improvised non-verbal communication. When communication is conducted between people of different cultures who do not share a symbolic system, the *X* portion of the intercultural model represents whatever improvised system they devise to make contact.

As we shall see in the section on contracultural and interracial communication, the important distinction between intercultural communication, contracultural communication, and interracial communication is the relationship of those individuals who are communicating. In intercultural communication situations, individuals are strange to each other; they have had a relatively separate historical development. As such, they tend to communicate more or less as equals.

Interracial Communication

Model II applies to interracial communication and to what we term "contracultural" communication. We shall first apply it to the interracial communication situations found now in the United States. Circle *A* represents the dominant power structure. In the case of the United States at present, *A* refers to white America and includes the physical, social, and psychological space occupied by white Americans, referred to as A_1.

Model II

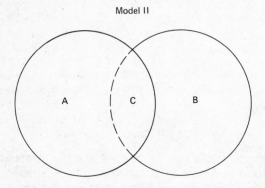

Circle *B* represents nonwhite racial groups as they exist in their purest form, uninfluenced by the structure of white America. For example, B_1 (the individual who occupies the physical, social, and psychological space of *B*), could be the immigrant Japanese *before* he reaches the shores of America, or the Mexican *abuela* [grandmother] who was brought to the United States by her family to dwell in the ethnic shelter of an East Los Angeles barrio. She speaks no English and may have created her own pure and unaffected racial subculture. There is some doubt, however, whether one may dwell in the United States and still be unaffected by the white structure. It is possible that B may exist only on its native soil or as an idealized concept in the mind of C_1.

Circle C represents the experience of being a racial minority in a white-dominated structure. It is the physical, social, and psychological space allotted to the nonwhite American. C_1 (and C_2, C_3, etc.) are the individuals confined to that space, the ethnic Americans (e.g., Mexican American, black American, Japanese American). The line of C transversing A is broken, not to suggest the possibility of C_1 ever entering into A, but to demonstrate that the size of C is elastic; it may vary depending on the whim of A, and, to a certain extent, on the tenacity of C in remaining close to B. For example, when Congress passes certain civil rights legislation, it enlarges the size of C. Such expansion of C into the domain of A, however, is under the control of A; the outside limit to which C can intrude on A is dictated by A.

On the other hand, C could, by its own choice, choose to remain small and closer to B. Certain Mexican American barrios, for example, have attempted to keep Mexican culture intact by speaking Spanish and generally preserving Mexican customs rather than adopting white Anglo-Saxon customs. The size of C will also vary depending on which group we consider as occupying C at any given time. Assume, for example, that C_1 represents black America and C_2 represents Mexican America. C_1 may be larger than C_2 because, at least until recently, black America has depended more on white America for its culture (e.g., language, customs) than has Mexican America.

Certain assumptions can be drawn from Model III. First, a member of C can never totally move within the realm of A. This is at present true in white-dominated America. Despite the thrust toward integration, white America has tenaciously maintained a portion of A into which, on the basis of color, nonwhite Americans may not enter. As long as a member of C can be identified as a nonwhite, he cannot pass into that portion.

On the other hand, a member of C can move within his allotted space of C and also within B, unless he has rejected or has been rejected by B. That is to say, a Japanese American is relatively free to return to Japan and drop his designation as a Japanese American if he desires. Though his ethnic minority experience in

Model III

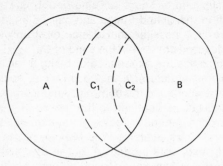

the United States may cause him certain problems of accultura-
tion within his new environment, in most cases there are few or
no legal or social barriers preventing a member of C from entering into B.

A third and significant assumption for interracial communication
is that a member of A can never become a member of C. A white
American, despite his good intentions, can never fully contem-
plate the experience of being a racial minority in the white-dominated country. Communication, therefore, between members of A
and members of C, or between white and nonwhite groups, is
highly difficult because of this lack of shared experience. The
outstanding characteristic of communication between members of
A and C (interracial communication as opposed to international
or intercultural communication) is that the existence of C (a segregated physical and psychological space dictated by A) causes
hostility and resentment on the part of its members; therefore,
tension and strain arise in any attempts at communication between
individuals in A and C.

On the other hand, communication between C_1, C_2, C_3, C_4, etc.
(black Americans, Mexican Americans, Japanese Americans),
stands a better chance of positive response because all these nonwhite groups, to some degree, share C. Although their C's may
vary in size, they all have experienced being a racial minority in a
white-dominated culture. Sitaram calls communication between
C's *minority communication.*[9] Because the terms "minority" and
"majority" are relative, based on one's system of classification,
and because the term "minority" tends to elicit abrasive reactions
among those who regard themselves as minorities in the United

States but majorities in the world, we prefer to call communication between *C*'s *interethnic communication*. Groups also included in the *C* classification of interracial communication in the United States are the native Americans (Eskimos, Indians, and Hawaiians) who have been forced into *C* space by the white structure.

Contracultural Communication

Contracultural communication occurs when the model of intercultural communication becomes transformed, through continued contact of cultures and the imposition of one culture on the other, into the model of interracial communication (Model IV). In other words, what began as a simple egalitarian interaction between two strange but relatively equal cultures becomes a colonial relationship in which one culture is forced to submit to the power of the other. The *X* of the intercultural model, that area of shared

Model IV

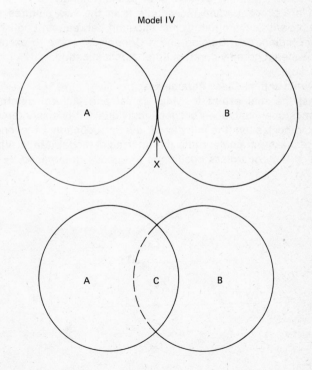

or improvised means of communication, becomes the *C* of the interracial model, an area in which individuals are relegated to a position and their mobility to move out of that position is dictated by a dominant structure. When Columbus first landed on the shores of the New World, for example, he undoubtedly engaged in intercultural communication with the natives he encountered. He improvised a system (e.g., he exchanged gifts). As colonization progressed, however, white Spaniards came to occupy *A* space and allowed certain Indians (from *B*) to form a *C* group. Had the Indians maintained control and enslaved the Spaniards, according to our theory, the Indians would then have occupied the *A* circle, with the Spaniards relegated to *C*. (And those Spaniards remaining safely in Spain would have comprised the *B* circle.)

The interracial model, then, also describes contracultural communication. As long as a power relationship exists between cultures in which one has subdued and dominated the other, a *C* circle exists; as long as a *C* area exists, hostility, tension, and strain are present when individuals from the two cultures communicate with each other. Communication between an Englishman and an Indian, or a Belgian and a Congolese, serve to exemplify what is meant here by contracultural communication.

Economic and/or Class Parameters

To test the real extent to which racial and cultural differences influence communication between individuals, it is also interesting to hypothesize on the effects of the introduction of economic and/or class parameters into the interracial model (Model V). Because in America class position is frequently determined by eco-

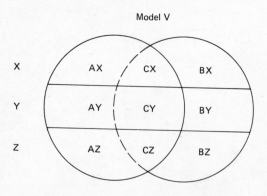

Model V

nomic position, let us, for the sake of discussion, combine the two, and consider X the highest, Y the middle, and Z the lowest socioeconomic class. An AX individual in our society would be someone of the caliber of Nelson Rockefeller or Richard Nixon (with Nixon as a rather new member of X and Rockefeller as a comfortable inheritor of position X): A CX in our society might be Thurgood Marshall or Edward Brooke. A BX would be a Japanese financier from Tokyo or a prime minister from Ghana.

Several interesting questions arising from such a structure could be translated into testable hypotheses for future research. For example, would Richard Nixon be more comfortable with and successful in eliciting a desired response from CX Edward Brooke (a fellow Republican, though black), an AY (middle-class clerk), or an AZ (poor coal miner)?[10] Would an American banker (AX) have a more successful business transaction with an African industrialist (BX) than he would with an American black capitalist (CX)? Do tensions and strains in interracial communication resulting from the very existence of area C diminish as an individual member of C climbs the socioeconomic ladder from Z to X, or do tensions take other, more subtle forms of expression? (It should be pointed out at this time that a member of C has upward mobility in this model; he may move from Z to X, but he still has no lateral mobility to the left; that is, a CX can still not become an AX, or even an AZ, for that matter.) These are just a few of the many questions suggested by the introduction of a socioeconomic parameter.

White Ethnic Parameters

One of the misleading assumptions of the interracial model thus far has been in the classification of all members of A as one unit. From the nonwhite point of view, all whites are very much alike in the structure of our society. They do, by virtue of their color alone, enjoy many benefits and advantages that nonwhites do not. On the other hand, ethnic differences exist between those occupying the A space in the model. Attempting, for example, to place Jews within the model of interracial communication poses a problem. The majority of C members (black Americans for example) perceive Jews as white and as a part of the white power structure. In fact, much black hostility against whites is aimed specifically at the Jew, because often the Jew is spatially the closest to the black. Yet the white society does not altogether regard the Jew as a member of the A group, and the Jew himself

Model VI

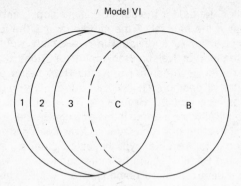

tends to identify at times with the more oppressed nonwhite groups. It seems appropriate therefore to add another dimension, that of white ethnic groups, to the interracial communication model. For example, in model VI we have arbitrarily divided *A* into three slices (it could conceivably be divided into as many slices as there are ethnic groups in the United States). The closer the *A* slice is to *C,* the more tenuous is its position in the *A* circle. Jews, for example, would occupy position 3, that closest to the realm of *C.* Slice 2 might be occupied by Irish, Polish, and Italian Catholics, and slice 1 would most likely be reserved for white Anglo-Saxon Protestants.[11]

A Multidimensional View

Model VII is a rather complex attempt to include all racial, ethnic, social, and economic variations in their various combinations that influence the manner in which individuals in a complex society can interact. The *ABC* parameter represents racial groups. The *XYZ* parameter represents socioeconomic class. The 1-2-3 notation in the *A* circle represents white ethnic groups (the higher the number, the less the group is regarded by the *A* circle). The 1-2-3 notations in the *C* circle have no values placed on them; they simply represent different nonwhite groups (e.g., CX_1 might represent a wealthy black man, whereas CX_2 might represent a wealthy Japanese American). The numbers denote the difference between the two racial groups. Circle *B* is not divided into complex ethnic subdivisions, because the focus of this chapter has been primarily on racial and ethnic compositions that structure human interaction in the United States.

Model VII

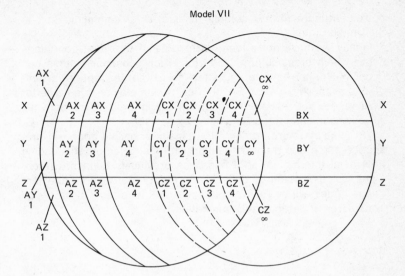

SUMMARY

We have attempted in this chapter to present certain definitions and theoretical structures within which we can view the complex phenomenon of intercultural and interracial communication. We have distinguished between international communication (communication on a political level between representatives of nations), intercultural communication (communication between individuals of different cultures with no previous colonial relationship), contracultural communication (communication between individuals of different cultures in which one culture has superimposed its values on the other and created a dominant–submissive relationship), interracial communication (communication between whites and nonwhites in the United States with nonwhites occupying a marginal position in the society and thereby introducing resentment and resultant strain into the interaction), and interethnic communication (communication between members of various nonwhite groups who have shared the experience of being a racial minority in a white-dominated structure).

We have also suggested how the added dimensions of economic class stratification and the multiethnic composition of the white power structure further complicate interracial communication in the United States.

Finally we have not attempted to present the ideal conditions under which cross-cultural and cross-racial communications can occur but rather have turned attention to the description of conditions as they now exist. Such a description may enable us better to diagnose the causes of communication breakdown between various conflicting forces in a complex society.

With this structure in mind, the remainder of this book will present research and theories dealing with major factors influencing interracial interaction, as it has been previously defined. Stereotypes, values, attitudes, beliefs, role theory, perception, and language codes will be related as causes and as effects of problems arising from interracial communication.

Activities

1. For one week, carefully read newspapers and magazines, and watch television news broadcasts. Identify, from contemporary events, examples of: (1) international communication, (2) intercultural communication, (3) contracultural communication, (4) interracial communication, (5) interethnic communication. Who were the participants in each? What were the chief characteristics of each form of communication? How did these various incidents differ from each other?
2. Describe an interracial communication situation in which you have participated. Do you regard it as a positive or negative experience? Why? What attitudes and emotions do you have when you think of engaging in interracial communication? In intercultural communication?
3. Where would you locate yourself within the described model of interracial communication? How do you think that position affects your behavior in interracial settings?
4. How would you change and/or improve on the models presented in this chapter?

NOTES

1. Dean C. Barnlund, *Interpersonal Communication: Survey and Studies* (Boston: Houghton Mifflin, 1968), p. 5.
2. Ibid., p. 18.
3. Ibid., p. 19.
4. Ibid., p. 20.
5. David Berlo, *The Process of Communication* (New York: Holt, Rinehart & Winston, 1960), p. 5.
6. Cf. Franklin Fearing, "Toward a Psychological Theory of Human Communication," *Journal of Personality,* 22 (1953): 71–88; C. Shannon, "A Mathematical Theory of Communication," *Bell System Technical Journal,* 27 (1948): 379–423; Bruce Westley and Malcolm Maclean, Jr., "A Conceptual Model for Communication," *Journalism Quarterly,* 34 (1957): 31–38.
7. K. S. Sitaram, "Intercultural Communication: The What and Why of It" (International Communication Association, Division V: Intercultural Communication Division, Minneapolis, Minn.,7–8 May 1970), p. 3.
8. Ibid., p. 2.
9. Ibid., p. 7.
10. Milton Rokeach, in *Beliefs, Attitudes, and Values* (San Francisco: Jossey, Bass, 1968), pp. 62–81, suggests in his findings on race, attitudes, and interpersonal choice that individuals are more likely to choose as partners those who hold common beliefs with them rather than those who are of the same color. This study was conducted only in the North, which may have influenced its validity. Rokeach also states that discrimination is institutionally sanctioned.
11. Certain religions tend to be associated with given ethnic groups, for example, Italian Catholics. Although religion could be introduced as an entirely separate parameter in the model, we have decided, for the sake of brevity, to combine ethnic background and religious affiliation into one graphic structure.

2

Perception, Prejudice, and Interracial Communication

A basic tenet of relativist philosophy and modern psychology is that every human being has his own reality, which, in varying degrees, may or may not correspond to the "objective" or "real" world. Walter Lippmann refers to this phenomenon when he discusses "the world outside and the pictures inside our heads."[1] At the heart of every interracial encounter is the sum of the "personal realities" each communicator brings to the communicative event. To understand why races interact as they do, we must first understand the basic principles whereby all men and women, regardless of race or ethnic background, absorb experience from their environment and make that experience personally meaningful. The phenomenon that explains this variance between what an individual may regard as "real" and what is "actually real" is called *perception.*

PERCEPTION

Definition

"Perception may be defined as the process by means of which an organism receives and analyzes information."[2] This definition describes two events in which we participate when interacting with our environment. First, we "receive" information. This reception refers to sensation or the process by which information comes to us through our senses.[3] As humans, however, we do more than just receive or sense stimuli; we also analyze what we sense. Such an analysis process has two components: attention and organization.[4]

The process of attention demonstrates that among the myriad of elements in our world which we may taste, smell, see, hear, and touch, we *select* those that are most meaningful to us. Because we cannot possibly sense all there is to be received in the environment, we systematically choose those stimuli to which we will attend. Frequently our selection is such that in order to make sense of the various elements we have selected, we must engage in a process of *organization.* In this manner we translate the experience of our sense receptors into a "useful and consistent"[5] picture.

"Perception is an active, not a passive, process. It is one in which the perceiver adds his own meaning to the data provided by his senses."[6] In the process of perception, this "meaning" that we provide through the organization of our sense experience is primarily based on learning, motivation, and social and personality factors.[7] As Bartley suggests: "Perceived objects are not existent entities in the outside world . . . Hence, in studying perception, we are studying what it is that the organism experiences, not what the physical world contains or is made up of."[8]

In his classic work *Public Opinion,* Walter Lippmann heavily emphasizes the disparity between what men perceive and what really exists. "In all these instances, we must note particularly one common factor. It is the insertion between man and his environment of a pseudo-environment."[9] He calls these "pseudo-environments" (or perceptions, according to Bartley) "fictions." "By fictions, I do not mean lies. I mean a representation of the environment which is in lesser or greater degrees made by man himself."[10] Lippmann goes on to state:

A work of fiction may have almost any degree of fidelity, and so long as the degree of fidelity can be taken into account, fiction is not misleading. In fact, human culture is very largely the selection, the rearrangement, the tracing of patterns upon, and the stylizing of what William James calls the "random irradiations and resettlements of our ideas."[11]

Krech and Crutchfield, in their definition of social perception, also emphasize the environment man creates for himself and its possible dissimilarity to the actual world:

Social perception does not consist of a series of discrete and unrelated observations; we integrate the discrete observations into a unified impression of the "complete personality," even inventing attributes when necessary, to fill out this complete impression.[12]

The process of human perception thus involves a reception (or sensation) of environmental elements based on the selection and

arrangement of certain stimuli into meaningful patterns. Such mean-
ingfulness is in great measure determined by personal, social, and
cultural learning and personality predispositions. Perceptions are
representative primarily of our physical and psychological states
as individuals rather than indicative of the absolute characteristics
and qualities of the perceived objects.

Factors Influencing Selectivity in Perception

It has been suggested that one of the outstanding characteristics
of the process of perception is its selectivity. Two sets of factors
tend to determine which of the elements in our environment shall
be selected and which shall be ignored. The first series of factors
that affects our selection "seems to depend upon the structure of
the stimulus situation and to produce much the same effect on all
observers."[13] Sometimes aspects of the perceived object tend to
command our attention and determine what we will see.

The first factor in the perceived object that tends to demand
attention is the quality of *intensity:* We tend to perceive the intense element rather than the weak. A shout is more effective in
gaining one's attention than a whisper. The old saying, "The
squeaky wheel gets the grease," refers to this intensity phenomenon. In terms of interracial communication, many "militants," in
justifying some of their rather intense tactics, suggest that society
never heeded their complaints or problems until public attention
was forced by extreme actions or stimuli.

Another quality of a perceived object that tends to demand attention and hence selection is *contrast.* Objects that stand out
from the background, items that appear to be different from the
norm, are selected for perception. Many revolutionary movements
seem purposely to select symbols that directly contrast with those
of the establishment to gain attention. Patterns of dress, grooming,
and social behavior at odds with those of the larger society have
drawn interest and even concern with regard to the youth culture.
Krech and Crutchfield suggest a common interracial implication
of this quality of contrast:

Some Americans believe that Negroes are unintelligent. When such
Americans meet a Negro of obvious intellectual achievement, they may
tend to *over*-estimate his intellectual capacity and see him as an excep-
tionally bright person. Here we have an instance of the perceiver of
attributes of an individual being affected by his group membership in
the direction of *contrast.*[14]

Finally a third quality that draws attention to the perceived object is *repetition*. A tune is catchy because it has a memorable rhythm, or it has a lyric that is repetitious and easy to remember. The notion that a statement repeated often enough tends to be believed has long been a basic tenet of persuasive communication. Such a tendency explains the effectiveness of slogans in catching the attention of the public: "America, love it or leave it," and "Power to the People" are good examples, because their constant repetition has made them stand out from the daily mass of communications.

The second set of factors that determines the selection of stimuli in the environment for perception is far more important in terms of its implications for interracial communication. Factors in the perceiver himself determine his selection of objects and his incorporation of those objects into a meaningful unit.

One characteristic in the perceiver that will determine what objects in his world he selects to observe and how he interprets those observations is past experience or learning. Although the effects of learning and past experience on selective perception and its impact on interracial communication will be expanded in the next chapter, on stereotypes, the following instance of intercultural interaction will serve as an example of the impact that learning can have on perception:

A Commission of African natives (Swazi) saw a large city for the first time when they visited London. Of what they saw there, what impressed them most was not the tall buildings, the speed of traffic, or the pomp and circumstance of the Court, but the sight of the London bobby directing traffic at a busy intersection. Among the Swazi, raising the arm is a sign of friendly greeting. Seeing this familiar gesture with its dramatic consequences in a strange setting was a very impressive experience.[15]

If past experience has taught us that fire is hot and burns, we will tend to select and perceive fire as a potential threat. Likewise if past experience or learning has taught us that certain peoples with certain characteristics will endanger us, we will select them from the mass of people with whom we interact and avoid them.

Another factor inherent in the perceiver which affects his selection and perception of external objects is motivation. The deprivation or lack of satisfaction of basic physiological drives and needs (to be further discussed in the chapter on values) puts the individual in a motivated state and has an enormous impact on what he selects to perceive. When a person finds himself in the physio-logical need state of hunger, it is very difficult to think of anything else but food. If he is driving, he tends to notice food advertise-ments and restaurants. When the need to eat is great enough, even the filthiest diner appears desirable. Women who desperately want to have children or who are pregnant frequently have testified that they tend to see nothing but babies, baby-associated objects, and other pregnant women.

The more ambiguous the stimulus, of course, the more learning and motivation play a part in the selection and interpretation of events. If, for example, a man who has been taught that Mexicans steal sees a dark-looking man running out of a store with a tele-vision set, he might interpret that experience as a Mexican man stealing. If, on the other hand, he is close to the store in ques-tion, and sees a well-dressed chicano carrying a television set to his car with the aid of the owner of the store, his past experience and learning will have less impact on his interpretation of the event.

Basic Perceptions

Contrary to our previous discussion, certain innate perceptions or patterns of analysis of sensory input appear to require no learn-ing or previous experience with the object. In order to determine which perceptions are basic and which must be learned, studies have been conducted with pigeons who were raised with their eyelids sewn shut. When their sight was restored, the birds tended to demonstrate abnormalities in perceptual behavior, displaying unusual postures as if disoriented in space. Similar studies, con-ducted with rabbits and chimpanzees, also point to the importance of learning in perceptual behavior.[16]

An important line of evidence, however, has been developed pointing to the possibility of certain innate perceptions. Studies have been conducted on congenitally blind persons whose sight has been surgically restored.[17] Such studies found that individuals perceive figure-ground relationships immediately after having their sight restored in much the same manner as do sighted sub-jects. The perception of geometric forms such as circles, squares, and triangles, however, is poor following surgery, suggesting that these perceptions must be learned.

The most interesting finding of these studies in terms of inter-racial communication is that early perceptions of the congenitally blind with restored sight tend to be dominated by *color*. This suggests that the ability to distinguish colors may also be innate. Consequently a child need not be taught that there are people of different colors; that recognition, according to Kimble,[18] is instinctual. The child must be taught, however, that there are qualitative values placed on colors. These qualitative values are not instinctual but learned. As we shall see later in this chapter, it is not the recognition of differences that constitutes prejudice but rather the manner in which we regard and respond to these differences.

First Impressions and the Persistence of Perceptions

Regarding social perception, which of course is the basis of interracial communication, we begin to form an integrated impression as soon as we observe anything about a person. "Out of a wealth of stimuli, the perceiver selects only the more salient ones upon which he builds his first impressions."[19] As pointed out previously, this "saliency" will depend on the cultural norms of the perceiver, his immediate emotional and motivational states, and/or his role relationship to the perceived person. An older conservative, for example, on viewing a younger person might select long hair as one of the features of importance in regarding the youth's appearance, whereas a younger person might not notice the long hair of his peer.

Once we have formed this "integrated impression," later observations will be influenced by our first perception; hence the stability of first impressions tends to be circular. The first impression of a person determines our behavior toward him. That person, in turn, behaves in a manner consistent with our behavior, and this consequently reinforces our initial impression. For example, if a white person perceives a black person as hostile and responds to his own perception with defensiveness or hostility, the black communicator will tend to respond to the white communicator's response with hostility. The first impression of the white communicator is then verified, perhaps a self-fulfilled prophecy. The black communicator may have been hostile from the outset, or he may have been friendly. The white communicator's predisposition to select any feature that could be interpreted as hostility, however, almost predestines the black communicator to grow into the hostile expectation of the white.

"The fixity of impressions of people is notorious, even in the face of contradictory evidence."[20] As explained in the next chapter, stereotypes are furthered by the selective filtering of evidence. In perceiving people we organize perceptions to relate people to subgroups and subgroups to larger groups, that is, we categorize. Then we set about to preserve our impressions. There are several means by which we attempt to maintain the integrity of original perceptions in the face of evidence at odds with our predisposition.

First we operate on the principle of constancy. If a person says or does something that is inconsistent with our original perception, we perceive him as insincere; we don't trust him. The concept of "perceived insincerity" will be developed further as it is related to communication between the races. The following example explains how it functions in general communication situations:

Suppose you believe that the political leaders of a certain foreign nation have a policy of war and aggression and suppose that you were to listen to one of their diplomats, on the podium of the United Nations, appealing for peace and good will. Under these conditions you may "perceive" all kinds of indications of insincerity in his speech, "cynical smiles," a "sneering tone," etc. You will interpret what you hear as "diplomatic double talk," and your original perception of him as an aggressive warlike person will remain unchanged. An external stimuli pattern (his appeal for peace and good will) which is inconsistent with a well-established precept has been so absorbed as to permit a constant perception of the diplomat to remain.[21]

If we determine that the individual who is not fulfilling our first impression or general expectation of members of his particular social group (racial, ethnic) is, in fact, sincere or does possess qualities that we do not ordinarily expect to find in members of his group, we also tend to engage in a separation of subsystems. We set people apart as exceptions to the rule. "Jacob Javits is a good man, but he is hardly representative of Republicans, in general," or "Edward Brooke cannot be regarded as indicative of the black population," are examples in which we account for the exception by excluding him from our generalization. In this way first impressions remain unthreatened and we do not allow individual qualities to interfere with our preconceived perception or stereotype of the group.

Kelly verified the powerful effect that preconceptions can have on actual perception and first impressions of individuals.[22] In his experiment two groups of MIT students were given different biographical accounts of an instructor who was to address them. To one group this instructor was described as "cold, industrious, critical, and practical"; to the other group he was described as "warm, industrious, critical, and practical." Both groups were then combined into one class and observed precisely the same performance by the instructor. The "warm" group of subjects rated him as "warm, considerate, informal, sociable, and humorous." The "cold" group described him as "self-centered, formal, and humorless." Fifty-six percent of the "warm" group participated in the class discussion and only 32 percent of the "cold" group did. Yet both groups were responding to the same person at the same time. In a real-life setting, if the students had responded to the instructor in a cool fashion, it is possible that the instructor would have responded coldly and reinforced the students' expectation.

Because we interact with other individuals, our perceptions affect not only our own behavior but may also affect the personality and behavior of the perceived person. In the chapter on roles we will see how our expectations can dictate how others behave toward us and hence reinforce our perceptions.

PERCEPTION AND PREJUDICE

We have seen that perception is selective and, in part, based on learning and motivation. Within the context of an interracial communication situation, one of the most important motivational characteristics affecting an individual's selection and organization of stimuli (i.e., his perception of the communication event) is racial and/or ethnic *prejudice.* In order to grasp fully the significance of the understanding of perception to the study of interracial communication, we must approach *prejudice* as the crucial link.

Definition of Prejudice

Originally derived from the Latin noun *"praejudicium,"* prejudice means simply a judgment based on previous decisions and experiences. In this early form the term had no pejorative meaning. As the word evolved into the English "prejudice," it acquired the meaning of a judgment formed before due examination and consideration of the fact, that is, a premature or hasty judgment.[23]

Finally "the term acquired also its present *emotional* flavor of favorableness or unfavorableness that accompanies such a prior and unsupported judgment."[24]

According to Gordon Allport, one of the primary traits that distinguishes "prejudice" from ordinary prejudgment is its resistance to change in the light of contradictory evidence. "Prejudgments become prejudices only if they are not reversible when exposed to new knowledge . . . A prejudice, unlike a simple misconception, is resistant to all evidence that would unseat it."[25] We grow emotional when our prejudices are attacked; yet we can discuss and rectify ordinary prejudgments without emotional resistance.

Prejudice is an attitude or a predisposition to respond to a certain stimulus in a certain manner. As Saenger suggests, "Prejudices, like all attitudes, may motivate us to act in a friendly or hostile way toward the objects of our prejudice, depending upon the nature and intensity of our feelings."[26] Simpson and Yinger go on to state that as an attitude, prejudice constitutes a *tendency* to respond. It may never develop into overt action toward the members of the group being judged in this manner, if the situation never presents itself.[27] They further emphasize that "prejudice involves not only prejudgment, but misjudgment as well. It is categorical thinking that systematically misinterprets facts."[28]

Finally, and perhaps most important to interracial communication, it should be noted that the objects of this "categorical thinking" and "misjudgment," are other individuals.

Ethnic prejudice is an antipathy based upon faulty and inflexible generalization. It may be felt or expressed. It may be directed toward a group as a whole, or toward an individual because he is a member of that group . . . The net effect of prejudice, thus defined, is to place the object of prejudice at some disadvantage not merited by his own conduct.[29]

But whereas prejudice and discrimination are related, they are not to be equated. Discrimination is the overt enactment of prejudice, "the differential treatment of individuals considered to belong to a particular social group."[30]

We shall refer to prejudice then as an emotional predisposition to respond favorably or unfavorably to a group of people or to an individual who represents such a group. This predisposition, being resistant to change and little affected by contradictory evidence, dictates our perception and hence is intrinsic to the attitudes we bring to any interracial encounter. Such a predisposition also dictates what features of the interracial communication situation we select, how we organize these features, and how we respond to our own synthesis.

Prejudice and Differential Perception

We have suggested that perception involves the selection and organization of stimuli from the environment. The very term "selection" suggests that stimuli differ and hence are distinguishable. Recall that "color" was viewed as an innate perception; we do not have to learn to distinguish between colors; we do so automatically. All this simply suggests that on a social level perception of visible differences between people is a natural and not necessarily hostile phenomenon.

Allport, in *The Nature of Prejudice,* suggests examples of obvious differences that distinguish groups of human beings: sex, age, skin color, cast of features, gestures, prevalent facial expression, speech or accent, dress, mannerisms, religious practices, food habits, and names. "All human beings show differences in appearance."[31] In discussing perception of human differences, Young suggests:

One of these [differences] is the awareness of color itself, another is the odor which frequently Orientals find unpleasant in the white man, or the white man, in turn, finds unpleasant in the Negro.[32]

It is not difficult to see how, through generalizations such as this regarding the differential perception of body odor, rigid stereotypes are formed. This process will be discussed in the next chapter.

Just as perception of differences is a natural and not necessarily prejudiced phenomenon, so is the sense of comfort brought about by being exposed to and surrounded by people like ourselves. It is also a natural or instinctual phenomenon to experience a sense of uneasiness when exposed to the strange or exotic.

Regarding the perception of differences, Allport states: "If there is any foundation for group prejudice, it lies in this hesitant response that human beings have to strangeness . . . If the familiar is good, then strangeness must be bad."[33] Yet both Allport[34] and Young[35] agree that the natural and automatic perception of differences and the accompanying "instinctual" fear of strangers are not sufficient to build extreme racial and ethnic prejudice. Although it is natural to select differences among people and to experience certain fears of some perceived differences, prejudice, with all its societal impact, must come from forces stronger than these; two major factors—culture and personality—influence the development of prejudice.

The Derivation of Prejudiced Perceptions: Culture and Personality

A distinction is frequently made between the process of adopting a specific prejudice and developing a generally prejudiced orientation toward the world. According to Allport: "A child who adopts prejudice is taking over attitudes and stereotypes from his family or cultural environment."[36] He goes on: "There is also a type of training that does not transfer ideas and attitudes directly to the child, but rather creates an atmosphere in which he develops prejudice as a style of life."[37] The first process described is that of the cultural derivation of prejudice. Later chapters will reflect directly on this process, whereby the individual in the society is culturally conditioned into the acceptance of certain values, attitudes, beliefs, role expectations, stereotypes, and language behavior. In this chapter we shall emphasize the personality that develops prejudice as a "style of life."

Studies have indicated that certain styles of child training are more conducive than others to the formation of a "prejudiced personality." Harris, Gough, and Martin, in an interview with the mothers of prejudiced and unprejudiced children, found that mothers of children in each group held significantly different views of child rearing and appropriate child behavior.[38] They found that mothers of prejudiced children far more than mothers of unprejudiced children held that:

1. Obedience is the most important thing a child can learn.
2. A child should never be permitted to set his will against that of his parents.
3. A child should never keep a secret from his parents.
4. They preferred children who were quiet to those who were noisy.
5. In the case of temper tantrums, they believed they should teach the children that two can play by getting angry themselves.[39]

"The child learns that power and authority dominate human relationships, not trust and tolerance. The stage is thus set for a hierarchical view of society."[40] Else Frenkel-Brunswik in "A Study of Prejudice in Children" further describes the "ethnocentric child" as one whose parents tend to lack genuine affection, are preoccupied with status, and place great pressure on the child to conform to strong parental discipline. The child, unable to express hostile feelings to his parents, displaces these aggressive tendencies onto his peers in a "bully" fashion.[41]

Eugene and Ruth Hartley investigated a sample of male students at City College of New York and described the characteristics of what they termed the "intolerant personality."

. . . an unwillingness to accept responsibility, acceptance of conventional mores, a rejection of "serious" groups, rejection of political interests, and a desire for groups formed for purely social purposes, an absorption with pleasure activities, a conscious conflict between work and play, emotionality rather than rationality, extreme egocentrism, interest in physical activity, the body, health. He is likely to dislike agitators, radicals, and pessimists. He is relatively uncreative, apparently unable to deal with anxieties except by fleeing from them.[42]

Allport suggests that the prejudiced person suffers a repression of his basic instincts, which results in: (1) an ambivalence toward parents, (2) an extreme moralistic view of the world, (3) a tendency to dichotomize everything into good and bad or black and white, (4) a need for definiteness and a low tolerance level for ambiguity, (5) a desire for order which results in a drive toward institutionalism, and (6) a strong tendency toward authoritarianism.[43] He describes his portrait of the prejudiced personality:

Underlying insecurity seems to lie at the root of the personality. The individual cannot face the world unflinchingly, and in a forthright manner. He seems fearful of himself, of his own instincts, of his own consciousness, of change, and of his social environment. Since he can live in comfort neither with himself nor with others, he is forced to organize his whole style of living, including his social attitudes, to fit his crippled condition. It is not his specific attitudes that are malformed to start with; it is rather his own ego that is crippled.[44]

A quite different personality profile is presented by these researchers with regard to the "tolerant" or "liberal" personality. Frenkel-Brunswik describes the "liberal child" as one with a greater orientation toward love than toward power, attributable to the greater affection he has received from his parents. This child feels freer to disagree openly and to resent his parents; he is thus more independent of his parents and has less need to displace hostility.[45] In their collegiate sample, Hartley and Hartley found:

The relatively tolerant personality in this type of collegiate sample is likely to exhibit some combination of the following characteristics: a strong desire for personal autonomy associated with a lack of need for dominance, a strong need for friendliness along with a personal seclusiveness, a fear of competition, a tendency to placate others along with a lack of general conformity to the mores.[46]

Allport also attributes specific characteristics to "tolerant personalities." He states that they tend to come from more permissive homes rather than threat-oriented ones; they tend to be more liberal or radical politically (they desire changes in the status quo); they have more education (higher education is correlated with less intolerance, perhaps because of a lessening of insecurity as education increases); they have a greater empathic ability or the capacity to "put themselves into another person's shoes"; they have more self-insight; and they demonstrate a greater tolerance for ambiguity.[47]

Controversial pediatrician-psychiatrist-pacifist Benjamin Spock, in his book *Decent and Indecent,* also offers a dichotomized approach to the prejudiced personality. He tends to agree with the previous researchers that one can divide personalities on the basis of prejudiced tendencies and offers a political personality approach to the explanation of this dichotomy. He divides personalities into progressives (radical and liberal), "people who are ready to go to the roots of the problems of society in analysis and cure," and conservatives/reactionaries, those not involved with problems remote from themselves. Spock traces these diverse personality tendencies, as does Allport, back to childhood and claims that the profile of each stems from the adaptation of each type of personality to the basic injustice of being a child. The progressive as an adult, extends his sense of childhood injustice to all the injustices he perceives in the status quo and hence is a constant agitator for change. The conservative who, like the progressive, was an unsuccessful rival with his parents more completely identifies with his parents as an adult than does the liberal radical and experiences the "my father was right" syndrome. The conservative thus tends to maintain the status quo.[48]

With the exception of Spock's work, the majority of research done on the prejudiced personality was conducted between 1945 and 1954. Following the World War II exposure of atrocities that had been perpetrated by men on other men, American social scientists became fascinated with the composition of a personality that could allow such crimes against humanity. During this period Adorno constructed his famous F scale to determine Fascist leader and follower tendencies in the personality. This desire to discover the "monster" in mankind tended to lead researchers toward a simplistic dichotomized view of inherent prejudices. The research previously discussed in this chapter might lead to a belief that there are prejudiced personalities and nonprejudiced personalities and nothing in between; common experience would tell us otherwise. The research thus far has dealt not with general prejudice as the majority of people in society possess and experience it but with the "unbalanced" personality, which employs prejudice as a way of life. Not all those in our society who hold prejudice are "sick" personalities, and it would be dangerous to assume they are.

Prejudice, whatever its origin, affects perception which, in turn, affects the manner in which people interact racially. Prejudice can be transmitted culturally, by the norms and values of the society; and, as demonstrated before, it can be implanted in the personality based on the child's early relationship with and adaptation to authority and affection in the form of his parents or surrogate parents.

Because prejudiced attitudes can contribute to personality makeup and not be merely a culturally derived stereotype, the task of effecting productive interracial interaction becomes even more difficult. To establish such effective interaction, we must demand that society turn its attention to establishing child-rearing practices that will result in children with egos healthy enough to enable them to respond and relate to those different from themselves. It is beyond the scope of this book to dictate those practices or even to suggest how society might implement such child-rearing once a system could be agreed upon. All parents, however, depending on how they interact with their own children, have the capacity to aid in the development of a tolerant unbiased personality, or conversely, to help produce the kind of "crippled" ego that preys on those who are weak or different. A major problem in any interracial communication situation is, therefore, the combination of personalities involved in that interaction. And at the core of that personality formation is early childhood training and parental treatment.

Effects of Prejudice on Perception
We have thus far defined perception and noted how it is influenced by learning and motivation. We have defined prejudice and the prejudiced personality and have suggested that prejudice, whether induced through culture or personality, can affect perception. Because mutual perception of communicators is so intrinsic to the process of interracial communication, we shall view some of the effects of prejudice on perception.

In their studies on rumor transmissions, Allport and Postman deal specifically with aspects of the perceptual process; in fact, they delve into questions of interracial perception.[49] The rumor studies are particularly relevant to the study of interracial communication, because many interracial expectations are based on mouth-to-mouth transmission of secondhand experience rather than on expectations derived from firsthand experience; that is, much of what we believe about those of other races and ethnic groups is based on what relevant others have told us or on rumor.

The Allport-Postman rumor studies were designed to discover the processes involved in the transmission of rumors which cause each communicator to select certain elements of the rumor message, eliminate other elements, and, through a kind of distortion, recombine the remaining stimuli into a meaningful perceptual unit. In an audience of subjects several persons are asked to leave the room. A transparency that depicts a detailed situation is then projected to the remainder of the subjects. An audience member is assigned the task of describing the scene (employing at least twenty details) to a subject just called back into the room, and the first listener is asked to describe the scene to a second listener. A third subject is called, and so on, until the last of the subjects has repeated the story he has heard regarding a picture he has never seen.

In analyzing the results, Allport and Postman describe three processes involved in rumor transmission. The first is *leveling:* Given a large number of details, as rumors are transmitted from person to person, they tend to grow shorter and more concise.

Fewer and fewer details are mentioned. About 70 percent of the details were eliminated as six mouth-to-mouth transmissions occurred.[50] The second process in rumor transmission is *sharpening* or "the reciprocal phenomenon of leveling": Sharpening is "the selective perception, retention, and reporting of a limited number of details from a larger context."[51] The final process involved in rumor transmission is *assimilation:*

When we ask what it is that leads to the obliteration of some details and the pointing up of others, and what accounts for the transpositions, importations, and other falsifications that mark the course of rumor, the answer is to be found in the process of assimilation, which has to do with the powerful attractive force exerted upon rumor by the intellectual and emotional context existing in the listener's mind.[52]

Because we are dealing with the effects of prejudice on perception (and the resultant interracial communication), and because prejudice is basically an emotional prejudgment, we shall focus on Allport and Postman's findings regarding highly motivated emotional assimilation, or "assimilation to prejudice."

In their study, Allport and Postman showed a transparency of Figure 1 to their subjects and asked them to describe it. The listeners from the first round of descriptions in turn continued to describe this picture by word of mouth to other listeners. The results of this rumor transmission were startlingly different depending on the race of the subjects describing the picture. In over one-half of the trials with white subjects, at some stage in the series of reports, the black man (rather than the white man) in the picture was said to have the razor. White subjects systematically shifted the razor from the hand of the white man to the hand of the black man. Some subjects reported the black man as "brandishing" or "threatening" the white man with it.[53] At times the razor moved from the white man to the black man early in the rumor transmission; at other times the transfer came later in the sequence of reports.

The black subjects in this experiment, on the other hand, tended to deemphasize the racial character of the picture. They suppressed the fact that anyone in the scene was black, ignoring any stereotypic aspects of the black race suggested by the picture; for example, they did not mention that the black man was much better dressed than the white man. (Whites of the study had

Figure 1 Subway scene used in rumor experiments. (From Gordon W. Allport and Leo Postman, *The Psychology of Rumor.* Copyright 1947 by Holt, Rinehart & Winston. Reprinted by permission of Holt, Rinehart, and Winston, Inc.)

emphasized this detail.) Finally, *no* black subject spontaneously removed the razor from the white man's hand and transferred it to the black man's hand. The results of this study of interracial perception indicate a strong tendency to perceive (select, ignore, and rearrange) stimuli in the environment on the basis of racial prejudice.

To any interracial communication situation, then, we bring the capacity and predisposition to "perceive" based on a combination of what really exists "out there" and the set of expectations existing in "the world inside our heads." Our prejudices not only pre-condition us to perceive gross events in special ways but also to respond to specific communicators and communication messages in special ways. As we shall see in the next section, prejudice-governed perceptions and sensitized interracial expectations persisting in a face-to-face interracial communication situation comprise one of the major problem areas in the achievement of productive interaction between racial and ethnic groups.

SENSITIZED PERCEPTION IN INTERRACIAL COMMUNICATION

Selective perception, frequently governed by such motivations as racial and ethnic prejudice, tends to define and circumscribe the interracial communication process. Perception, being selective and interpretive, governs the behavior of interracial communicators. The process of *sensitization,* strongly related to selective perception, is a process that has developed through the exposure of members of different races to each other, usually under hostile circumstances. This has caused communication messages to be selected, interpreted, and responded to in a special way.

Psychological sensitization is not unlike physiological sensitization. In the purely physical sense a person becomes sensitized to an element in his environment; his tolerance for this element is decreased and may result, in a case of overexposure, in an extreme allergic reaction. This same tendency seems to occur psychologically in the process of interracial communication. Through exposure to a certain ideology, rhetoric, and/or social movement, we become sensitized to certain ideas and especially to certain words. Words that were once accepted in conversation with little or no emotional reaction are now selected and interpreted as intolerable and offensive.

A well-known example of the sensitization process can be found in the evolution of terms used (usually by whites) to refer to blacks. The terms "nigger" and "boy" used by whites in reference to blacks have, for the most part, always offended blacks. Other terms, however, such as "colored" and "Negro" have, until fairly recently, been used by whites in reference to blacks in an attempt to be polite and inoffensive. Contemporary black rhetoric stressing pride in blackness and independence from white domination has now rejected the terms "colored" and "Negro" as offensive, and exposure to this rhetoric has sensitized many blacks to regard whites who use these terms as "racists." Thus whereas the terms "colored" and "Negro" might once have caused no problems in an interracial communication situation, through the process of sensitization, these same terms introduced now by whites are selectively perceived and cause extreme "allergic" reactions in black listeners. A similar process is also occurring with the term

"Mexican American," which many members of this ethnic group are rejecting in favor of "chicano." A "chicano" who has become sensitized to the term "Mexican American" may become extremely upset if an "Anglo" persists in the use of that term within an interracial context.

The process of sensitization can cause the sensitized receiver to respond in various ways when he hears a member of another ethnic or racial group use a term that he perceives as offensive. He may "bristle" (have an extremely negative signal reaction), he may perceive the source of the communication as insincere, or he may experience simultaneous responses. We shall refer to statements that cause negative signal reactions as "bristle" statements and statements that cause the receiver to regard the source as insincere as "perceived insincerity" statements.[54] A bristle statement may still be perceived as being sincere. For example, if a white were to say to a black, "I don't trust colored people," the black may have an extreme negative signal response but still regard the speaker as sincere in what he says. On the other hand, some bristle statements are also perceived insincerity statements. The often-stated "some Negroes are my best friends" offends the black listener because he selectively perceives and negatively responds to the term "Negro" as opposed to "black" and will most probably be perceived as insincere by a black receiver. It should be noted that the concept of a perceived insincerity statement does not suggest that the speaker is really insincere but rather that he is perceived as insincere by the listener.

In a study conducted at UCLA of the communication problems existing in an ongoing interracial group,[55] the author asked each racial and ethnic faction to compose a list of bristle and perceived insincerity statements made by members of other racial and ethnic groups. An analysis of these lengthy lists demonstrates that most of the statements that caused negative and unbelieving perceptions and responses fell into one of five categories.

1. *Stereotypic statements*   "Stereotypic" statements tend to ignore individual differences between ethnic group members and emphasize generalized and/or exaggerated traits of the group. Blacks in the group, for example, listed as offensive statements such as "all colored people have good voices," "blacks have natural soul," "all blacks look alike," "niggers is always stealing," and "blacks are the grooviest people." Chicanos listed such

stereotypic statements as "all Mexicans are lazy," "Mexicans don't do well in school," and "Mexicans are loyal and will work for little money." Some stereotypic statements that the Japanese Americans in the interracial group resented were "Japanese are very hard-working," "how do you tell the difference between Japanese and Chinese?" and "Japanese are intelligent, courteous, and soft-spoken." The Indians also had stereotypic statements they regarded as offensive: "How, Chief," "do your people have trouble with alcohol?" and "do you live on a reservation?" It should be noted that not all these stereotypic statements are derogatory. They nevertheless induce a high emotional reaction in the interracial setting, because they deny the identity of the individual and place him, positively or negatively, within a larger structure that disregards his human uniqueness.

2. *Statements lacking sympathy with antiestablishment complaints*
A second series of bristle and perceived insincerity statements can be classified as those that show lack of understanding and sympathy with complaints various ethnic groups offered against the status quo. Examples given by the subjects were: "You have the same opportunities as anyone else," "I worked hard for what I have, you must do the same," "everybody is repressed by the system," "nothing happens overnight," "look at Willie Mays. He made it, so can you," and "what do you people want?" These statements indicate a typical lack of shared experience between white and nonwhite group members, as was discussed in Chapter 1.

3. *Condescending statements*   A third classification includes those bristle and perceived insincerity statements that are interpreted as revealing feelings of superiority on the part of the source toward the receiver. Verbal stimuli such as "boy," "kid," "son," "culturally deprived," and "minority" trigger negative signal responses. Statements made by whites indicating a desire to go into the "ghetto" to "raise the standards" or to aid the "culturally disadvantaged" were interpreted as condescending and produced extreme negative emotional responses in the various ethnic group members.

4. *Statements demeaning the women of an ethnic group*   Each ethnic group offered examples of statements that offended them because they to some degree insulted the females of the group.

Statements referring to the sexual attributes of black women or the desire of black men for white women produced extreme bristle responses. Chicanos resented the same kinds of statements directed at the sexual promiscuity of chicano females, and the Indians were violently offended by the use of the term "squaw." Comments reflecting on the moral standards of the women of the various groups were interpreted as reflecting on the power of the males of that group to protect their women. Any statements, then, dealing with interracial sex or the sexual attributes of female members of ethnic groups were extremely disruptive to the emotional atmosphere of the interracial group.

5. *Statements attempting to cross ethnic barriers*   The various ethnic groups listed statements made by "outsiders" which attempted to demonstrate familiarity with the customs and codes of their respective groups as offensive and insincere. Examples given by blacks in the nonverbal area were: attempts by whites to give the black power handshake or sign, to wear "natural" hair styles, and to dress in African garb. They also found verbal statements offensive in which whites employed such black expressions as "right on," "soul brother," and "sister" as well as the use of "we" by whites when addressing blacks. Chicanos objected to being addressed as "amigo" or "compadre" by non-chicanos. A major Indian complaint refers to the statement frequently made by whites: "I am part Indian myself."

Most of the above bristle and perceived insincerity statements were offered by members of various nonwhite racial and ethnic groups. White subjects were also asked to list those statements that elicited a negative signal response in interracial discussion. Most of their complaints seemed to be a reaction to the hostility directed at them by members of various nonwhite ethnic groups. They objected to being classified all as one, "the man" (a stereotypic statement). They also tended to perceive much of the revolutionary talk as insincere and did not believe that various ethnic group members were willing to "lay it on the line," as they claimed. Finally, they resented being blamed as individuals for the "sins" of the white race and having their attempts at interracial understanding classified as "armchair liberalism."

The process of sensitization, nurtured by selective perception, has produced many diverse problems in interracial communication. Many emotional outbursts and resultant tensions can be attributed to the use of some bristle and perceived insincerity statements and the frustration experienced by all group members, regardless of ethnic identity, in attempting to deal with such explosive reactions.

SUMMARY

This chapter has demonstrated that perception, the means of selectively receiving and organizing our experience, is at the core of any interracial encounter. Perception governed by an emotionally based attitude such as ethnic prejudice preconditions us to select certain elements in the environment and to "rearrange" reality. We bring our prejudices to the interracial situation, and we are prepared to see and hear those stimuli that will fulfill our expectations.

We have also seen that society and personality structure help to determine our prejudiced perceptions. Such perceptions provide an enormous yoke of confining predisposition under which we must perform in order to interact productively with those who are the victims of frequently mistaken expectations. Because communication is cyclical and processlike, we in turn are victims of the preformulated notions of others. In the next chapter, we shall examine the result of prejudice and selective perception, the *stereotype,* and the manner in which it functions as a barrier to effective communication between members of diverse racial and ethnic groups.

Activities

1. As a class exercise, present an ambiguous picture of an interracial situation. Allow each class member to write a brief description of the situation as he or she has perceived it. Compare these descriptions to determine if class members of different races have perceived the picture selectively and differentially.
2. Conduct the Allport-Postman rumor experiment in class. If the

transparency is not available, use a large drawing of the bus scene. Divide the class into racial groups and observe the differential responses based on race.
3. What incidents and influences in your background do you think aided in developing or diminishing your racial prejudice? To what degree do you think your own perceptions are governed by your prejudices? Can you cite some of your prejudiced perceptions?

NOTES

1. Walter Lippmann, *Public Opinion* (New York: Macmillan, 1957), p. 3.
2. Brian Fellows, *The Discrimination Process and Development* (Oxford: Pergamon, 1968), p. 218.
3. Gregory A. Kimble, *Principles of General Psychology* (New York: Ronald, 1956), p. 104.
4. Fellows, op. cit., p. 5.
5. Ibid.
6. Kimble, op. cit., p. 160.
7. Ibid.
8. S. H. Bartley, *Principles of Perception* (New York: Harper & Row, 1958), p. 22.
9. Lippmann, op. cit., p. 15.
10. Ibid.
11. Ibid., p. 16.
12. David Krech and Richard S. Crutchfield, *Elements of Psychology* (New York: Knopf, 1959), p. 667.
13. Kimble, op. cit., pp. 145–146.
14. Krech and Crutchfield, op. cit., p. 669.
15. Kimble, op. cit.
16. Ibid., p. 160.
17. D. O. Hebb, *The Organization of Behavior: A Neuropsychological Theory* (New York: Wiley, 1949).
18. Kimble, op. cit., p. 161.
19. Krech and Crutchfield, op. cit., p. 667.
20. Ibid., pp. 667, 668.
21. Ibid., p. 670.
22. Ibid., p. 669.
23. Cf. Sir James A. H. Murray, ed., *A New English Dictionary*, vol. 7, pt. 11 (Oxford: Clarendon, 1909), p. 1275.

24. Gordon Allport, *The Nature of Prejudice* (Cambridge, Mass.: Addison-Wesley, 1954), p. 6.

25. Ibid., p. 9.

26. Gerhart Saenger, *Social Psychology of Prejudice* (New York: Harper & Row, 1953), p. 4.

27. G. E. Simpson and J. M. Yinger, *Racial and Cultural Minorities* (New York: Harper & Row, 1965), p. 19.

28. Ibid., p. 15.

29. Allport, op. cit., p. 9.

30. Robin Williams, Jr., "The Reduction of Intergroup Tension," *Social Science Research Council,* Bulletin 57 (1947): 37–38.

31. Allport, op. cit., p. 131.

32. Kimball Young, *Social Psychology* (New York: Appleton-Century-Crofts, 1956), p. 501.

33. Allport, op. cit., p. 130.

34. Ibid., p. 131.

35. Young, op. cit., p. 501.

36. Allport, op. cit., p. 297.

37. Ibid.

38. D. D. Harris, H. G. Gough, and W. E. Martin, "Children's Ethnic Attitudes: II: Relationships to Parental Belief Concerning Child Training," *Child Development,* 21 (1950): 169–181.

39. Allport, op. cit., 298.

40. Ibid., p. 299.

41. Else Frenkel-Brunswik, "A Study of Prejudice in Children," *Human Relations,* 1 (1948): 295–306.

42. Eugene L. Hartley and Ruth E. Hartley, *Fundamentals of Social Psychology* (New York: Knopf, 1952), p. 710.

43. Allport, op. cit., p. 396.

44. Ibid.

45. Ibid., p. 305.

46. Ibid., p. 710.

47. Ibid., p. 426.

48. Benjamin Spock, *Decent and Indecent* (New York: McCall, 1970), pp. 137–145.

49. Gordon Allport and Leo Postman, *The Psychology of Rumor* (New York: Holt, Rinehart & Winston, 1947).

50. Ibid., p. 75.

51. Ibid., p. 86.

52. Ibid., p. 100.

53. Ibid., p. 111.
54. Cf. Jack L. Daniels, "The Facilitation of Black-White Communication," *Journal of Communication* 20, no. 2 (1970): 135–136.
55. Andrea L. Rich, "Some Problems in Interracial Communication: An Interracial Group Case Study," *Central States Speech Journal* 22 (Winter 1971): 228–235.

3

Stereotypes and Interracial Communication

DEFINITION OF STEREOTYPE

Stereotypes profoundly affect human behavior, particularly inter-racial communication, for they determine how we react to and interact with environmental stimuli. The term "stereotype" is employed extensively by laymen and scholars from a wide variety of disciplines; yet definitions of "stereotype," not only numerous and diverse, are at times seemingly contradictory.

Many of the viewpoints generally expressed in present-day literature regarding stereotypes originated as far back as 1922 with Walter Lippmann, one of the first to define and employ the construct of the stereotype. Lippmann characterizes stereotypes as: (1) a means of organizing images, (2) fixed, simplex impressions, and (3) salient features chosen to stand for the whole. He also notes that stereotypes are convenient, time saving, and necessary; without them, man would have to interpret each situation as if he had never before experienced it. Lippmann further states that a stereotype is a defense mechanism; an attack on it is an attack on a person's feelings and sentiments.[1]

Most scholars concur with Lippmann on the above points. Lippmann's other generalizations regarding stereotypes, however, have recently been open to question. He suggests, for example, that stereotypes refer to things as well as people; most theorists, on the other hand, discuss stereotypes only in terms of the way groups of people are perceived. Further, Lippmann describes stereotypes as those classes of "pictures in our head" that are essentially negative and unfavorable representations of other groups of individuals. More recent authorities, however, maintain that some stereotypes are highly favorable. Klineberg, for example, cites a specific case to support this view:

Written with the collaboration of Dennis M. Ogawa.

. . . it is true that the dominant group will recognize certain desirable qualities in the subordinate group and may go so far as to develop positive or favorable stereotypes. For example, . . . although white people of Robeson County, North Carolina, express their dislike of the Croatan Indians who live among them in much the same terms as they express their feelings toward Negroes, they will usually say, "but there is one thing we can say for them, they are hard workers, they save their money, and they are the best tobacco farmers in the world."[2]

Lippmann also asserts that stereotypes are essentially incorrect representations and hence are undesirable. This pejorative definition is still maintained, to some degree, by certain scholars. S. I. Hayakawa identifies stereotypes with "widely current misinformation" and with "traditional nonsense."[3] Simpson and Yinger note that stereotypes, as commonly applied, contain distortion and error and embrace negative traits.[4] Gordon Allport suggests that "some stereotypes are totally unsupported by facts; others develop from a sharpening and over-generalization of facts."[5]

This view of stereotypes as essentially inaccurate perceptions is not universally held by scholars researching the phenomenon of stereotyping. Although they admit that some stereotypes do involve gross error, many researchers stress that not all stereotypes are contrary to fact. Rokeach, for example, states that ". . . a person's stereotype may contain an element of truth in it. . . ."[6] Some authorities suggest that there is *usually* a "kernel of truth" in stereotypes. Supporting this contention are Dudycha,[7] Remmers,[8] Meenes,[9] Seago,[10] Den Hollander,[11] De Bie,[12] Schrieke,[13] and Buchanan and Cantril.[14] Solomon Asch emphatically insists that stereotypes include valid judgments. He doubts not only the insight gained when treating stereotypes as "wrong judgments" but also the value of reserving the meaning of the term to "designate subjective and uncritically held ideas about social groups."[15]

The definition of "stereotype" as employed in this book does not exclude either of the above viewpoints; rather it embraces both. It recognizes that stereotypes may be either relatively true or false, negative or positive.[16] Our definition also includes those characteristics often agreed on by most theorists, that is, stereotypes as relatively simplex, general, rigid cognitions of social groups that blind the individual to the manifold differences among members of any group—racial, ethnic, age, sex, or social class.[17] In short, stereotypes are viewed as relatively representative or nonrepresentative of actual conditions, favorable or unfavorable, general, fixed, simplex cognitions attributed to a group of people.

THE PERPETUATION OF STEREOTYPES

Stereotypes are stubbornly resistant to change. Once such cognitions have been formed by the individual, they tend to persist. If stereotypes frequently contain misinformation, how do they survive the individual's experience? How does a man who believes that all Jews are stingy account for the generous Jew he may meet?

According to Lippmann, when a system of stereotypes is well fixed, attention is called to those facts that support it and diverted from those that contradict it. Such a process is termed "selective perception." Consciously, and more often unconsciously, people are impressed by those facts that fit "the pictures in their head."[18] Being preconditioned to perceive selectively, kindly people discover reason for kindness, malicious people reason for malice. Capitalists see one set of facts, socialists another. If one expects, on any given occasion, to find a white racist, a violent black, or a lazy Mexican, he undoubtedly will find one. Individual differences tend to be overlooked in such situations, for a person guided by fixed preconceptions does not study a man and judge him to be bad; he merely sees a bad man. He selectively—consciously or unconsciously—perceives the data supporting his stereotype and selectively ignores those aspects of the perceived individual that contradict his expectation. Gordon Allport describes this phenomenon of selective perception and selective forgetting:

When a Jew of our acquaintance achieves a goal, we may say quite automatically—"The Jews are so clever." If he fails to achieve the goal we say nothing—not thinking to amend our stereotype. In the same way, we may overlook nine neat Negro householders, but triumphantly exclaim when we encounter the slovenly tenth, "they do depreciate property."[19]

Many problems erupting in interracial communication settings can be attributed to this individual tendency to perceive selectively and perpetuate stereotypes. For example, police–community relations boards, arising throughout the country to deal with the growing split between the police force and the inhabitants of ghetto areas, are increasingly dismayed. They find that despite their efforts to train police in methods of handling ghetto residents more diplomatically and despite vast public relations campaigns to change the image of the police in such areas, the slogan of "Police Brutality" persists. So strong in the minds of the people is the stereotype of the "cop" as an exploiting outsider that any attempts made by the police to be kind and solicitous are selectively ignored. Likewise, many police, conditioned to perceive certain "types" as threatening, tend to treat all residents with certain characteristics as suspect. The cycle of hostility and tension continues. Both the source and the receiver in such communication situations view each other not as individuals with unique traits which must be discovered, but as cardboard cutouts, one-dimensional objects with no mystery and no humanity.

FUNCTION OF STEREOTYPES

It should not be concluded that stereotyping is totally deleterious to human interaction. The individual's need to stereotype is not based solely on ignorance and bigotry. In the most general sense, we stereotype to conserve energy. The vast array of stimuli that bombard us constantly must be structured in order for us to function in the midst of possible chaos. We cannot be expected to know beforehand all the special traits of each individual with whom we will ever come in contact. Yet we are expected to act with decorum at all times; in other words we must know what others expect of us. In order to accomplish this, we categorize people into various groups (racial, ethnic, social, political, sex, hair color, etc.) and generalize a series of traits for each group. We thus enable ourselves to predict how this multitude of "others" will behave in various situations. By making events in human interaction predictable, we lend order to our lives and reduce the tension inherent in facing the unknown.

Stereotyping becomes dangerous when it blinds us to the individuality of those with whom we interact; when relying on preconceptions as fact, we cease to search for multidimensional qualities of individuals. The line between order and rigidity is thin indeed.

ORIGINS OF STEREOTYPES

We are not born with "pictures in our heads." Stereotypes have to be learned; they do not suddenly appear through instinct. Stereotypes become established in our consciousness in several ways. First, we learn to stereotype through personal experience. Having interacted with a member of a different racial, ethnic, religious, or social group, we generalize to other members of that group a trait or series of traits that have positively or negatively impressed us. We condition ourselves to look for these same characteristics in future encounters with members of the stereotyped group, and through selective perception we find those traits. Our stereotype thus grows in strength and rigidity as we selectively verify it for ourselves. The stronger such a stereotype becomes, the less likely we are ever again to acknowledge characteristics that may contradict our preconception.

We also develop stereotypes "secondhand" through the experience of "relevant others." Just as we learn language, values, attitudes, and beliefs from our family, teachers, and friends, so do we tend to adopt their stereotypes. This tendency to adopt the stereotypes of others is particularly strong when one has not had sufficient personal experience with the stereotyped person or group to contradict the cognition passed on by the influential model figure. Even if one fervently desired to remain open-minded in all his social encounters, chances are that he would have been unconsciously conditioned to find traits that others have suggested to him as characteristic of the group with which he interacts. It is true that many young people reject the stereotypes their parents have held and passed on to them; such a rebellion involves a crucial and painful "unlearning" process whereby the children must consciously uncover data that contradict their previously held conceptions.

Finally we learn to stereotype through the mass media. Books, newspapers, magazines, motion pictures, radio, and television present us with generalizations about most groups in society. The sheer volume of stimuli aimed at establishing such rigid images has made the media increasingly more important as a source of generally held stereotypes. Although it is beyond the scope of this book to analyze fully the various racial and religious stereotypes created and furthered by the mass media, we shall mention briefly the impact of selected works.

Books in America were one of the earliest forms of public expression to project stereotypes. The now almost cliché "Uncle Tom" image so vehemently rejected by black militants was first offered by a white abolitionist, Harriet Beecher Stowe, in her work *Uncle Tom's Cabin.* The childlike and dependent qualities bestowed on Tom by the condescending abolitionist still disturb the black population. Another American classic, *Gone with the Wind,* persisted in offering the image of the black as the faithful servant, grateful to his master and incapable of caring for himself.

The power of newspapers to project stereotypes is even greater than that of books, because timeliness and wide circulation enable the press to move vast segments of the population to emotional fervor. Newspapers have the power to create negative pictures of selected "enemies" necessary to enable a population to justify the ultimate communication breakdown, war. They bring mysterious strangers to us, of whom we know and generally care nothing, and reveal to us images so threatening that we feel we act in all righteousness when we destroy for "self-protection." Newspapers have not limited stereotyping to foreign peoples; they have also stereotyped our own citizens. During World War II, newspapers, prompted by public officials, were instrumental in raising public opinion to such a pitch that a majority of the racial population of Japanese Americans in Cailfornia was moved physically from their homes and businesses to relocation centers. Newspapers, as well as other media, helped to instill such fear in the population of California against Americans of Japanese ancestry that the total destruction of the civil rights of a group of American citizens met with little or no resistance. This incident illustrates the impact of blind stereotyping in its most offensive form. Similarly in Nazi Germany it was the redefinition of Jews as nonhumans that made possible the subsequent extermination of 6 million people.

The history of motion pictures in the United States is likewise a history of the projection and perpetuation of rigid cognitions of racial and ethnic groups. Blacks, through countless "plantation pictures," have consistently been portrayed as servants. The character of Step 'n' Fetch It, while earning millions for the black actor who portrayed him, fixed indelibly in the white mind the image of the shuffling, slow-moving, slow-talking, slow-thinking black man. The genre of Charlie Chan movies furthered some incredible racial stereotypes. It gave us Feet Do Your Stuff, the cowardly black man whose claim to fame was the facility with which he could escape challenging situations. Charlie himself was the victim of positive stereotyping. Very wise and very clever, he was a master at problem solving. To avoid fear that films had really produced a Chinese competitor for Sherlock Holmes, filmmakers were always careful to cast a white man in Charlie's role. Ironically the part of Charlie's number one son, always a dullard, was consistently played by a Chinese.

For many years miscegenation was a taboo in American films. More recent attempts to present this reality on film have resulted in some interesting casting and characterization. In the film *A Majority of One,* a potentially moving story of an older Jewish woman who becomes emotionally attached to a wealthy Japanese, the part of the Japanese was portrayed by Sir Alec Guinness, with the aid of artificial plastic epicanthic folds. This, coupled with Rosalind Russell's portrayal of the Jewish matron, greatly diluted the issue of miscegenation. A more daring project dealing with the same theme was *Guess Who's Coming to Dinner.* Here, however, the black character, about to marry a young white lady of considerable social standing in her community, suffers from reverse stereotyping. Instead of being developed as a realistic character, he is presented as a "super-black," beautiful, brilliant, and world-renowned.

In general, motion pictures in the United States have historically presented racial and ethnic group members as "types," positive or negative. Only whites have been consistently regarded as multidimensional characters. As the film industry begins to include members of racial and ethnic groups into the business of the cinema, perhaps viewers can look forward to increasingly more sensitive polyethnic portrayals. In the meantime the strength of the images projected by this powerful medium remains. From the inscrutable Asian foe to the Pancho Villa bandito, stereotypes projected through films continue to influence the manner in which diverse peoples interact with each other.

Perhaps the most powerful medium of all, reaching more people than any other, is television. A brief look at the history of television programming since its inception in the 1940s and early 1950s will demonstrate that television has focused primarily on entertainment about white America for white America. In most of television's series and playlets, racial and ethnic groups have until very recently been either ignored or presented in the most stereotypic fashion. In the early days of television, there were shows about blacks. Two outstanding examples are "Beulah" and "Amos 'n' Andy." Beulah was the faithful and highly responsible servant of a white family. She was wise, honest, loyal, and delighted with her work. She was everything white America wanted in a servant.

Furthermore, the stereotype was enhanced by Beulah's constant struggle to keep her ne'er-do-well boyfriend in line. He was smaller than she and was stupid. A television program such as this, innocent as it may have seemed in the days before protests attempted to enlighten us, probably did much to further the stereotype of the black woman as a self-satisfied subservient and of the black man as chronically irresponsible. The character of Lightening from "The Stu Erwin Show" was television's answer to Step 'n' Fetch It. In the mold, he was slow and docile. Bringing "Amos 'n' Andy" to television proved more of a problem, because the actors who created these characters on radio were white. Recast, however, with black actors, "Amos 'n' Andy" eventually came to the small screen. Aside from providing work for some black actors this show did little for the black segment of the population. Its humor was based on the inefficiency and stupidity of its characters, and again we find the henpecked oaf of a husband in the Kingfish and the strong force in his nagging wife, Sapphire. In 1966 CBS withdrew "Amos 'n' Andy" from syndication and overseas sale after several civil-rights groups protested that it was a distorted portrayal of Negro life in the United States. And there was Rochester of "The Jack Benny Show," a male Beulah, bright and witty, but still a servant.

Blacks were not the only racial group relegated to subservient roles in television. Asians were traditionally servants, such as Hop Sing in "Bonanza," the Chinese house boy Peter in "Bachelor Father," and Mrs. Livingston in "The Courtship of Eddie's Father." Indians were "faithful companions" or savage attackers but seldom were fully developed characters. Chicanos were almost totally ignored, except of course for the Cisco Kid and his "faithful companion," Pancho.

It should not be assumed from these examples that early television spent much time on racial and ethnic groups. For every show that presented even one stereotypic nonwhite character, there were dozens that simply ignored the fact that America is a multiracial, multiethnic society. The mainstay of American television, the situation comedy, the form that was to throw light and humor on situations from our daily lives, provides numerous examples of this racial sterility. Our Miss Brooks, an endearing and beloved teacher, had no black students; ethnic diversity did not exist at Madison High School. Joan Davis of "I Married Joan" never threw a pie at a chicano or a Japanese American. "Make

Room for Daddy," "Father Knows Best," "The Donna Reed Show," "December Bride," "The Life of Riley," "My Favorite Husband," "My Little Margie," "Life with Father," "Topper," "Ozzie and Harriet," and many others had no racial problems. The children in these shows never had nonwhite friends; there were never any black neighbors. It was not that the characters on these shows were bigoted. They were not bigoted; they were not unbigoted. They were simply oblivious. Anyone watching these shows as indicators of life in America would have to conclude that America had only white inhabitants.

Stereotypes, then, are formed through personal experience, through the passed-on experience of relevant others and through the influence of the mass media. They structure perception in such a way as almost to predetermine how one will interact. The views members of various racial groups hold of each other is thus crucial in terms of the effectiveness of interracial interaction.

RESEARCH ON INTERRACIAL STEREOTYPES

The following section is designed to present a sample of the kind of research that has been conducted regarding stereotypes and interracial communication. The methodologies employed are flawed somewhat by a lack of sophistication in design, but it is this very simplicity in the procedures that makes this form of elementary investigation into interracial communication stereotypes an excellent in-class tool and exercise for the discovery of communication stereotypes.

The studies were undertaken in two parts. The first, conducted and published by Dennis Ogawa in 1971, attempted to define the stereotypes white Americans hold of black, chicano, and Japanese Americans.[20] The second, conducted by Andrea Rich in 1972, sought to discover for the first time black perceptions of white, chicano, and Japanese American communicators.

Both portions of the study employed the Katz and Braly methodology for discovering stereotypes.[21] First a stereotype checklist dealing with ethnic communication characteristics was developed. Thirty white and thirty black UCLA undergraduate students were asked to list what they considered to be the communication characteristics of three major racial groups in the Los Angeles area. Whites were asked to list the "specific characteristics you think are typical of the communicative behavior of black, chicano, and

Japanese Americans." Blacks were asked to list typical communicative behavior of white, chicano, and Japanese Americans. The student lists were combined and supplemented with words from Katz and Braly's original list deemed relevant to this study and from the investigators' research into contemporary stereotypes found in newspapers, magazines, and books. The following fifty-seven adjectives were placed randomly to form the completed checklist:

hesitant	quiet	hostile
intelligent	quarrelsome	reserved
argumentative	conservative	nondirective
critical	arrogant	jovial
practical	concealing	inarticulate
submissive	aggressive	soft-spoken
meditative	uninvolved	humble
boastful	imaginative	conformable
ignorant	noisy	open
witty	directive	individualistic
industrious	passive	fluent
emotional	evasive	silent
efficient	conventional	responsive
suave	persistent	incomprehensible
resistant	ostentatious (showy)	talkative
methodical	obliging	rude
alert	radical	defiant
straightforward	loud	imitative
sensitive	courteous	nonmilitant

In the Ogawa portion of the study, the list was administered to 100 white UCLA undergraduates. In the Rich segment, the list was presented to 100 black residents between the ages of 18 and 25 living in the East Los Angeles ghetto. Those conducting the black portion of the survey were black research assistants who were able to overcome the natural reticence demonstrated by members of the black community in responding to surveys conducted by white scholars. Written instructions supplied to the subjects were:

Read through the list of words on page one and select those which seem to you typical of the communicative behavior of 1. white Americans (or black Americans), 2. Mexican Americans, and 3. Japanese Americans. Write as many of these words in the following spaces as you think are necessary to characterize the communication of each of these groups. If you do not find appropriate words on page one for all the typical characteristics, you may add those which you think are necessary for an adequate description.

A separate page for each ethnic group followed this paragraph of instructions in which subjects wrote in the traits they considered typical of communicative behavior of members of each of the races. On the completion of listing the traits, subjects were asked to review the three lists of words they chose and mark with an *X* the five words in each list that seemed most typical of the communicative actions of the racial group in question.

To determine the degree to which each of the groups was stereotyped, the study employed the Katz and Braly method for estimating degree of agreement. Had there been no patterning in the images the subjects held of the various groups, 28.5 (half) of the traits would have received 50 percent of the votes. On the other hand, if the subjects had agreed perfectly on the five traits typical of a group, 2.5 traits would have received 50 percent of the votes. It was thus reasonably determined that if thirteen or fewer traits received over one-half of the votes, a group could be considered stereotyped, for this sum would be far from a chance selection. One could deduce that even if the least degree of agreement were thirteen traits, some degree of uniformity exists, given in comparison, the 28.5 traits that would have occurred purely by chance. The fewer the number of traits, then, receiving 50 percent of the votes, the greater the degree to which a group is stereotyped.

Results
The results of the stereotype list administered to white subjects in the Ogawa portion of the study are presented in Table 1. This includes the twelve characteristics most frequently assigned to the three racial groups by the 100 Caucasian students. The table summarizes the traits that the subjects checked as the five most typical communicative characteristics of each group.

White Stereotypes of Black, Mexican, and Japanese Americans
Traits assigned to black and Mexican Americans by white subjects demonstrate a remarkably close resemblance. The first four traits attributed to both groups are almost identical, though the order differs.

Table 1 The Twelve Communicative Traits Most Frequently Assigned to the Three Ethnic Groups by 100 Caucasian UCLA Students

Traits checked (rank order)	Percent	Traits checked (rank order)	Percent
Black Americans		**Mexican Americans**	
Argumentative	40	Emotional	53
Emotional	35	Argumentative	32
Aggressive	32	Sensitive	25
Straightforward	26	Straightforward	19
Critical	26	Talkative	19
Sensitive	20	Intelligent	16
Ostentatious	19	Persistent	15
Defiant	17	Loud	15
Hostile	17	Courteous	14
Open	17	Hesitant	13
Responsive	17	Open	13
Intelligent	17	Critical	12

Traits checked (rank order)	Percent
Japanese Americans	
Intelligent	73
Courteous	60
Industrious	48
Quiet	42
Soft-spoken	36
Reserved	31
Sensitive	25
Efficient	25
Practical	23
Alert	21
Humble	19
Conservative	16

Table 5 The Least Number of Communicative
Traits that Must Be Taken to Include 50
Percent of the Possible Assignments for
Each Ethnic Group

Group (*rank order*)	No. traits required
Japanese Americans	7.15
White Americans	10.80
Mexican Americans	11.46

hold of whites in this segment and the image whites hold of blacks
as presented in the Ogawa portion of the study. Four of the traits
that blacks ascribe to whites, whites also ascribe to blacks: "emotional," "aggressive," "critical," and "ostentatious." Whereas any
one of these terms is not necessarily negative in connotative
value, taken together they seem to describe the existence of a
mutual contempt between the black and white communicators.
Further, although in the Rich segment blacks regarded whites as
"evasive," in the Ogawa portion, whites viewed blacks as "straightforward." That whites view blacks as straightforward is rather
ironic in the light of recent discussions and explanations of the
complex roles blacks have assumed in the presence of whites,
which in many ways do not reflect their true feelings and desires.[26]

Black Stereotypes of Mexican American Communicators
The Rich portion of the study determined that black perceptions
of Mexican Americans are similar to the white perceptions of
Mexican Americans as reported in the Ogawa segment.

black perceptions	white perceptions
emotional	emotional
radical	argumentative
talkative	sensitive
argumentative	straightforward
loud	talkative
aggressive	intelligent
sensitive	persistent
critical	loud
defiant	courteous
straightforward	hesitant
rude	critical
ostentatious	open

A comparison of these lists demonstrates that blacks and whites had a 50 percent agreement on the traits they attributed to Mexican American communicators. Both groups perceive chicanos as "emotional," "talkative," "straightforward," "critical," "loud," and "argumentative." The white stereotype of chicanos appears to be slightly less negative than the black view, since whites chose nonthreatening terms such as "courteous" and "hesitant," whereas blacks chose the opposite terms "rude" and "radical."

There are several explanations for the disparate views blacks and whites hold of chicanos and the seemingly negative preconceptions blacks hold of chicanos. It is possible that whites interact with chicanos under different conditions than do blacks or that both blacks and whites perceive chicanos as white, and hence blacks view them more negatively than do whites. A further explanation of the hostility revealed between blacks and chicanos in this study lies in the nature of the ghetto conditions in which blacks and chicanos coexist. Both groups (blacks and chicanos) share the same physical and psychological space allocated to them by the white society; thus in many instances they are forced to compete with each other for the favors of white society. Such competition may have created animosity, with racial and ethnic ties taking precedence over common economic-class problems.

It should be added that many groups of blacks and chicanos (especially in universities and colleges) would deny the existence of this hositility in an attempt to build a united front against the white establishment and to fight against allowing depressed conditions to split nonwhite unity. The empirical results of this study conducted among ghetto blacks, however, reveals that attempts at building unity of nonwhites has not yet diminished the negative preconceptions that the tested blacks hold of chicanos.

Others, seeing these results, have argued that adjectives such as "radical," "defiant," and "aggressive" do not necessarily have negative connotations for blacks. Indeed it could be advanced that those with these traits would be admired by blacks for their revolutionary posture. This argument has merit when one views certain of the traits out of context, but on examination of the total profile of adjectives chosen, it becomes apparent that the distinctly negative connotations of terms such as "rude" and "ostentatious" suggest that the list as a whole is reflective of a negative stereotype held by blacks of chicanos.

Black Stereotypes of Japanese Americans

The black response to the portion of the survey that focused on traits of Japanese Americans again demonstrates the transracial strength of stereotypes, because blacks of this portion of the study expressed approximately 66.6 percent agreement with the whites of Ogawa's segment regarding the views both groups held of Japanese Americans.

black perceptions	white perceptions
intelligent	intelligent
industrious	courteous
soft-spoken	industrious
reserved	quiet
nonmilitant	soft-spoken
quiet	reserved
courteous	sensitive
humble	efficient
submissive	practical
uninvolved	alert
sensitive	humble
passive	conservative
efficient	

Connotations of the adjectives chosen to apply to Japanese Americans by both black and white groups were generally positive with regard to overall societal values, with the blacks choosing a few negative (to them) political terms such as "nonmilitant" and "conservative." As we can see from Table 5, of all the groups tested the Japanese Americans again are the most strongly stereotyped with over 50 percent of the black respondents agreeing on 7.15 traits. Likewise, in the Ogawa portion, 50 percent of the white subjects agreed on only 4.75 traits.

Implications of Stereotype Research for Interracial Communication

The results of this study suggest that the stereotypes blacks hold of white communicators are so negative that, with the influence of selective perception reinforcing these negative views, productive interracial communication is rendered difficult, if not impossible, at times. The study also reveals a great lack of trust and empathy between blacks and whites in communication situations; the resultant interpersonal gap must be overcome if interracial communication is to occur without the disruption caused by antagonism and hostility.

The study demonstrated that stereotypes are so strong they cross racial and ethnic barriers. Such occurrences are not surprising when one recalls some of the ways in which stereotypes are developed. All groups in this country are subjected to the mass media of books, newspapers, magazines, motion pictures, radio, and television. Many stereotypes are learned and reinforced through these media, and membership in a given racial or ethnic group does not make us immune to their influence.

The tendency to rely on stereotypes to ease the difficulty of interacting with the unfamiliar is extremely strong for all humans, regardless of racial or ethnic identity. It is easier to draw on preconceptions when in doubt than it is to make the effort to seek out and know individuals. We program ourselves to categorize first and respond later. Although stereotypes are thus helpful in ordering the complexity of human experience, they interfere with meaningful interaction, because they predispose interaction between preconceptions rather than between the participants themselves.

Researchers and instructors in interracial communication must address themselves to the problem of overcoming the stifling effects of strong racial and ethnic stereotyping if multiracial and multiethnic communication is to occur. The unfortunate alternative to fighting the negative results of stereotyping is the acceptance of an even more polarized society where individuals are poised to do battle with the "windmills of their minds."

Activities

1. Describe in specific terms the fundamental racial and ethnic stereotypes to which you have personally been exposed through motion pictures and television.
2. What stereotypes do you recall from your experience with major literary works?

3. Do you personally hold any racial and/or ethnic stereotypes? What are they? Where did they come from? Have you ever seen any evidence to contradict them? How did such evidence make you feel?

4. Conduct a stereotype experiment in class such as the one described on pages 51–53.

5. Divide the class into a series of small (five or six persons) interracial discussion groups. With candor have all group members describe to each other how other members do or do not conform to the racial stereotypes of the various group members.

NOTES

1. Walter Lippmann, *Public Opinion* (New York: Macmillan, 1957), pp. 79–103.

2. Otto Klineberg, *Characteristics of the American Negro* (New York: Harper & Row, 1944), p. 17.

3. S. I. Hayakawa, "Recognizing Stereotypes as Substitutes for Thought," *Etc., Rev. Gen. Seman.* 7 (1950), 209.

4. G. E. Simpson and J. M. Yinger, *Racial and Cultural Minorities* (New York: Harper & Row, 1965), pp. 119–120.

5. Gordon Allport, *The Nature of Prejudice* (Cambridge, Mass.: Addison-Wesley, 1954), p. 190.

6. Milton Rokeach, *Beliefs, Attitudes, and Values* (San Francisco: Jossey, Bass, 1968), pp. 125–126.

7. G. S. Dudycha, "The Attitudes of College Students Toward War and the Germans Before and During the Second World War," *J. Abnorm. Soc. Psychol.* 35 (1940): 566–572.

8. H. H. Remmers, "Attitudes Toward Germans, Japanese, Jews and Nazis as Affected by the War," *School and Society* 57 (1943): 138–140.

9. H. Meenes, "A Comparison of Racial Stereotypes of 1930 and 1942," *J. Soc. Psychol.* 17 (1943): 327–336.

10. D. W. Seago, "Stereotypes Before Pearl Harbor and After," *J. Psychol.* 23 (1947): 55–63.

11. N. J. Den Hollander, "As Others See Us: A Preliminary Inquiry into Group Images," *Syntheses* 8 (1948): 214–237.

12. P. De Bie, "Representation du Benelux," *Bull. Inst. Rech. Econ. Soc.* 17 (1951): 637–710.

13. Schrieke, *Alien Americans* (New York: Viking, 1936).

14. W. Buchanan and H. Cantril, *How Nations See Other Nations* (Urbana: University of Illinois Press, 1953).

15. S. E. Asch, *Social Psychology* (Englewood Cliffs, N.J.: Prentice-Hall, 1952), p. 232.

16. Such a negative and positive characteristic has been noted by Allen L. Edwards, "Studies of Stereotypes: I. Directionality and Uniformity of Responses to Stereotypes," *J. Soc. Psychol.* 12 (1940): 357–366.

17. Krech, Crutchfield, and Bilachedy point out some of these same salient features, e.g., race, ethnic group, sex, in their discussion of stereotypes in David Krech et al., *Individual in Society* (New York: McGraw-Hill, 1962), p. 55.

18. Lippmann, op. cit., pp. 115–130.

19. Allport, op. cit., pp. 191–192.

20. Dennis Ogawa, "Small Group Communication Stereotypes of Black Americans," *Journal of Black Studies* 1 (1971): 273–281.

21. D. Katz and K. W. Braly, "Stereotypes of 100 College Students," *J. Abnor. Soc. Psychol.* 28 (1933): 280–290.

22. T. F. Pettigrew, "Racially Separate or Together," *J. Soc. Issues* 25 (1969): 48.

23. M. L. Kohn and R. M. Williams, "Situational Patterning in Intergroup Relations," *Amer. Soc. Rev.* 21 (1955): 164–174.

24. I. Katz, "Review of Evidence Relating to Effects of Desegregation on Performance of Negroes," *Amer. Psychol.* 19 (1964): 381–399.

25. Individual adjectives such as "emotional" do not necessarily suggest a negative connotation, but, viewed within the total profile of response, they tend to point to unfavorable attitudes.

26. Cf. Sam Greenlee, *The Spook Who Sat by the Door* (New York: Bantam, 1970).

4

Role, Culture, and Interracial Communication

INTRODUCTION TO ROLE THEORY

Definitions

Despite his protestations against tyranny and his constant agitation for individual freedom, man does not act as a free agent. Restraints on his total freedom of action are not primarily physical nor are they mainly political; rather they are for the most part social, imposed on him by the group with whom he lives and works. Shakespeare suggested that our world is a stage and that we are nothing more than actors. His metaphor hints at the phenomenon of social control, the set of expectations that we must fulfill in order to fit comfortably into the social environment.

The concept of "role," of man the actor,[1] is essential to the understanding of human social behavior. According to Turner, a role is:

A collection of patterns of behavior which are thought to constitute a meaningful unit and deemed appropriate to a person occupying a particular status in society (e.g., doctor or father), occupying an informally defined position in interpersonal relations (e.g., leader or compromiser), or identified with a particular value in society (e.g., honest man or patriot).[2]

"Role" differs from "status" in that it is not a position we can occupy; it is rather a set of behaviors that is enacted. A priest, for example, must act in a certain manner in order to satisfy the expectations others hold of him as a man of God. If he were to use profanity, steal from the poor, or physically attack an innocent person, he would betray the expectations of his parishioners and would most probably be relieved of his post. We expect mothers to love their children, fathers to provide for their families, teachers to set good examples for students, criminals to harm victims, men to be strong and aggressive, and women to be gentle and passive.

When we fulfill the expectations of others regarding the roles attributed to us, we engage in "role playing," the actual enacting of the appropriate role behavior one perceives for himself. Role playing is not to be confused with "playing at a role." The latter is pretending—acting a role not necessarily appropriate to oneself. This dishonest form of behavior, pretending to be what one is not, differs greatly from role playing in which the individual simply acts in the manner others expect of him. In the process of human interaction the individual also engages in "role taking" or imagining temporarily to be another person. In this manner, we put ourselves into the roles of others in order to determine what the "relevant others" expect of us; hence we are able to adjust our behavior accordingly. When interacting with the "boss," for example, we ask ourselves, "If I were an employer, how would I want my employee to behave?" Once we determine the answer, and if we desire to remain in our present position of employment, we act according to the expectations we attribute to him. We engage in "role taking" then, for prediction, to determine how others expect us to behave.

Role taking should not be thought of in the same terms as the sociodramatic exercise of "role reversing." Whereas role taking is a spontaneous, sometimes unconscious aid in human interaction, role reversing is an artificial, though frequently useful, attempt to gain understanding of others in an interpersonal group. In role-reversing exercises individuals dramatically enact the behavior they perceive as being relevant to the role of another in the group. Thus in an interracial group blacks may portray the behavior they perceive to be exhibited by whites, providing insight both for blacks in experiencing how it feels to be in a "white" position and for whites in seeing how blacks perceive them.

Finally the phenomenon of "role strain" is worth noting. We do not play one single role throughout our lifetimes. Frequently we must enact many. A father may also be a businessman or a senator, a mother may be a teacher or an actress, as well as a parent. Each role has distinct expectations associated with it, and on occasion these expectations conflict. A professional woman who is also a mother experiences role strain; she is at once expected to be efficient in her work and to be at home caring for her children. She cannot do both and hence experiences tension and conflict. If the strain becomes too intense, she is frequently forced to give up one of the roles or fulfill it less completely. The more complex society becomes, the greater will be the role strain experienced.

Development and Function of Role Expectations

We learn to enact roles and to expect the proper enactment of roles from others for much the same reason as we stereotype. Social living is complex living. We cannot interact with so many individuals without social guidelines. Roles make behavior predictable. We know how we must behave and how others must behave; we are also aware of the consequences of refusal to fulfill social expectations. Roles limit the number of unknowns we must face and hence diminish the anxieties of social interaction.

Predictability and ease of interaction are not the only reasons that societies employ roles as guidelines for behavior. Fulfilling the demands of role expectation is a method of maintaining social order and control. Individuals gather together in groups. Through group consensus or "mutual understandings" and common assumptions underlying cooperative endeavors,"[3] this conglomerate of individuals begins to develop a "culture," a series of "conventional understandings, manifested in art and artifact, which characterize particular groups."[4] Common understandings of appropriate behavior, once they are universally accepted, begin to form the "norms" of the group, the standards by which the members of the group judge the desirability or undesirability of the actions of the various community members. The maintenance of individual behavior within the confines of group expectations constitutes "social control."[5]

If an individual refuses to abide by the norms of the group, he is subject to social sanctions, by which "the conduct of erring individuals is brought back into line with accepted usage."[6] Social sanctions, like group norms, vary from society to society. In Hawthorne's *The Scarlet Letter,* the heroine's punishment for breaking the norms of the community (committing adultery) was a scarlet "A" placed on her chest for all the community to see. In more modern times society's scorn for such behavior is perhaps more subtle, but it still exists, nevertheless, in gossip networks and varying degrees of social ostracism by the group.

ROLE PHASES IN INTERRACIAL COMMUNICATION

Subcultural Roles

Group norms regarding role expectations are not constant in time nor are they shared consistently by all members of an inclusive society. Subcultures of a multiracial and multiethnic nature exist in complex societies. A subculture is a "normative system of groups smaller than a society."[7] A subculture gives "emphasis to the ways these groups differ in such things as language, values, religion, diet, and style of life from the larger society of which they are a part."[8] The diagram below exemplifies our concept of the manner in which the members of the dominant society (*A*) interact with members of the nonwhite subculture *(C)*.

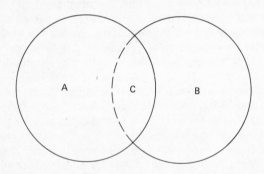

In our definition of a subculture (as opposed to a "countercul-ture," which will be defined shortly), nonwhite *C* members main-tain the dominant *A* group's definition and perception of the status quo. As a *C* member, the nonwhite places no pressure on the dominant white culture to change in any way; rather the *C* mem-ber accepts the physical and psychological space allotted to him by *A*. In modern parlance those who accept the terms "Negro" and "Mexican" for themselves instead of "black" and "chicano" are seen as members of a subculture instead of a counterculture because they have accepted the traditional means of self-definition originally dictated by the dominant white society. The more radical nonwhite counterculture members regard those in the nonthreaten-ing and nonaggressive subculture as "sellouts to the establish-ment" and as "Uncle Toms."

Just as society has defined role expectations for occupations and sexes, so has it defined the "appropriate" behavior it expects of members of its various racial and ethnic groups. These role expectations are closely related to the stereotypes that members of the larger community hold of the subcultural groups. For example, as the previously described research suggested, a common stereotype held of the Japanese American is that he is "quiet," "efficient," and "industrious." This stereotype results in a Caucasian's set of expectations regarding the behavior of the Japanese American. The Japanese American, knowing how he is expected to behave, fulfills that expectation, enacts the role, and thus reinforces the white stereotype of Japanese efficiency.

Interethnic interaction proceeds without difficulty as long as the role expectation of the larger community coincides with the role the subcultural groups perceive as appropriate for themselves. When the self-image of the group conflicts with the expectation of the larger culture, difficulties arise. Such difficulties have resulted in the "marginal man" syndrome. Here individuals are "called upon to play roles which consist of contradictory claims and obligations."[9] A black intellectual, for example, finds himself misunderstood by members of ghetto communities; yet he is not fully accepted by other intellectuals because of his racial identity.

Communication, then, between a subcultural *C* group member and a member of the dominant white culture is characterized both by role playing and by playing at a role. Members of subcultural *C* groups interact in a role-playing fashion when the *C* member does not question the role expectations of the white society and fulfills them unconsciously. Such might have been the case with ex-slave Frederick Douglass when he interacted with his masters *before* he became enlightened and learned that slavery was not a necessary and natural state of being. When through reading he discovered that others regarded slavery as evil, he began to question the expectations the white society held for him.

The literature of interracial relations tends to indicate, however, that genuine role playing on the part of *C* toward *A* is relatively rare; most subcultural *C* group members, even though they do not desire to change the status quo, do experience a conflict between the manner in which they perceive themselves as human beings and the manner in which white society expects them to behave.

In order to survive this conflict of role expectations, many members of racial and ethnic groups find themselves playing at a role in the presence of members of the larger community in order to satisfy the expectations of the general culture. Privately, however, they do not regard the behavior they exhibit publicly as a true indicator of their own personalities. For many years in the South, for example, it was expected that a black man should move off the sidewalk to let a white man pass, a behavior demanded by the white community to demonstrate and emphasize the supposed inferiority of the black race. In order to avoid conflict and even physical retaliation, blacks complied with that expectation. The negative sanctions for not fulfilling the role expectations of the white community were severe indeed, as the history of white lynchings of black offenders well demonstrates.

A more humorous example of playing at a role by subcultural group members in the presence of individuals of the larger community is presented in many scenes of the television comedy, "All in the Family." Here Lionel, a bright black college student, plays a distinct role in the presence of Archie, the middle-aged bigot. Archie expects Lionel to speak with a stereotypic southern black accent and to be dim-witted. Lionel, always laughing behind Archie's back, fulfills that expectation.

Sam Greenlee, in his chilling novel *The Spook Who Sat by the Door,* makes one constantly aware of the painful efforts of members of subcultures to discern and fulfill the expectations of the larger white society:

Carter Summerfield had sat in his office all morning, worried and concerned. He sensed the senator was not pleased with his performance and could not understand why. Summerfield had sought desperately to discover what it was the senator wanted to hear in order that he might say it, and was amazed to find that the senator seemed annoyed when his own comments were returned, only slightly paraphrased. In all his career as a professional Negro, Summerfield had never before encountered a white liberal who actually wanted an original opinion from a Negro concerning civil rights, for they all considered themselves experts on the subject. Summerfield found it impossible to believe Senator Hennington any different from the others.

He had spent the morning searching for the source of the senator's displeasure until his head ached; the handwriting was on the wall and Summerfield knew his job was at stake. He must discover the source of displeasure and remove it. Perhaps he should wear ready-made clothes; had the senator somehow seen him driving the Lincoln, rather than the Ford he always drove to the office? It was essential never to have a more impressive car than one's boss. He told all his newly integrated Negro friends that. Had anyone discovered the encounter with the white girl in Colorado Springs when he had accompanied the senator on a trip to the Air Force Academy? He had been certain he had acted with the utmost secrecy and discretion. But he had known even then that it was a stupid move which might threaten his entire career.[10]

Countercultural Roles

When a subculture finds itself at odds with overall society, when "a series of inverse and counter values"[11] (values opposed to those of the surrounding community) is created, then a counterculture is formed. The counterculture represents "norms that arise specifically from a frustrating situation or from a conflict between a group and the larger society."[12] The diagram below demonstrates our concept of one type of countercultural role enactment

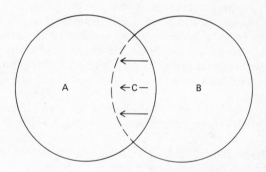

Countercultural Role Type I: Aggression

and communicative behavior. This diagram of the aggressive phase of countercultural interaction suggests that the countercultural nonwhite *C* member, unlike his subcultural counterpart, is most definitely pressuring the white dominant society (*A*) to change the status quo. This phase represents a concerted effort on the part of countercultural *C* members to change *A*'s attitudes, to open the physical and psychological space allotments, to change the dominant–submissive role definitions, to modify the institutions, and, in short, to revolutionize the interracial environment. This aggressive and self-assertive behavior based on a new countercultural role definition may be peaceful or violent. It may embody persuasive tactics or coercive means or both. Demonstrations, riots, marches, hunger strikes, boycotts, nonwhite voter registration drives, and elections all constitute countercultural expressions of aggression against the status quo of the white dominant society.

The existence of countercultures places immense strain on the larger society, for there is little or no consensus between the surrounding community and the counterculture. As the counterculture pressures the larger society by refusing to accept its norms and thereby detracts from the predictability and order of social interaction, social disorganization tends to result. Thomas and Znaniecki suggest that "social disorganization is an incidental part of social change."[13] They suggest that social change, or the transformation of social structures, is not likely to occur without a temporary breakdown of consensus. The implications of social disorganization for any form of human communication are vast, because human interaction relies strongly on the ability of the source of the communication to predict the response his message will induce. The inability to make such predictions can prove disastrous, inasmuch as the individual communicator is rendered impotent in his ability to avoid dangerous or threatening encounters. Contemporary social disorganization in the refusal of many members of racial and ethnic countercultures to conform to the role expectations of the larger society has resulted in hostile and threatening interaction situations between members of the culture and the counterculture.

The greatest difficulties in interracial and interethnic interaction thus arise when the subculture becomes a counterculture, and the racial and ethnic group members refuse to continue to play at a role for the sake of avoiding conflict with the general culture. The personal strain and tension caused by the necessity of constantly playing at a role results in deep frustration for the racial group member and eventually evolves into hostility and aggression. Much of the basis of racial and ethnic revolutions throughout the country involves the rejection by the various countercultures of the notion that it is necessary to conform to the larger culture's expectations. By refusing to enact the roles dictated by the general society, these countercultures attempt to alter society's expectations. Such efforts are designed to force the larger community to accept the role definitions of the counterculture.

Communication then between a white *A* and an aggressive countercultural *C* is characterized usually by a refusal on the part of *C* to fulfill *A*'s behavioral expectations and an attempt on the part of *C* to enact a role dictated by his *own* counterculture. There are cases, however, in which aggressive countercultural *C* group members do play at a role, but the motivation is quite different from that of subcultural group *C* members playing at a role. Whereas subcultural members fulfill the behavioral demands of the dominant society in order to maintain personal security and preserve a kind of peace, countercultural group *C* members may engage in playing at a role in order to facilitate aggressive and revolutionary ends. By *pretending* to accept the dominant culture's behavioral expectations, such a countercultural group member presents a nonthreatening façade and throws his white receivers off guard. There is literary evidence, particularly black, of this duplicity in interracial communication. The entire plot of *The Spook Who Sat by the Door* is based on the ability of a black hero to enact so fully the role expectations of the white society that his white superiors have no notion of his plans to lead a nationwide racial revolution. From the gold cap he places on his tooth to the avoidance of the proper French pronunciation of fine wines, the protagonist totally captures the image his white "dupes" hold of the benign "Negro."

For the most part, however, the more revolutionary countercultures regard fellow *C* members who attempt to conform to the larger society's role definitions with some disfavor. Blacks, for example, refer to such conformists as "Uncle Toms." They call for more honesty in interracial interaction ("Tell it like it is!" "Give Whitey hell!"). Ironically this thrust toward honest interaction on the part of the revolutionary groups proves disruptive to interracial interaction, even though the quality of honesty is generally regarded as a positive attribute in interpersonal communication. Honesty, in this case, however, refers to the uninhibited expression of hostility, which is normally so threatening to the members of the larger community that they withdraw from the communication field entirely. The suggestion that some degree of "dissemblance" is usually necessary for the continuation of interpersonal communication seems relevant here.[14]

These countercultures have refused not only to conform to the role expectations of the general society; they have also formed new role expectations for themselves. The violent and hostile manners of expression frequently demonstrated in interracial interaction by more revolutionary racial group members have been referred to by some as "bravado rhetoric," a new role or set of behavioral expectations established by the countercultural group to intimidate some whites with whom they might interact. The assumption here is that the personal feelings of the hostile communicator toward the larger community member may not be as vehement as they appear but serve publicly to reinforce the values of the counterculture.

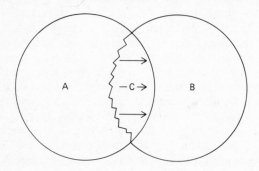

Countercultural Role Type II: Withdrawal

In this second type of countercultural syndrome, members of *C* totally reject *A* members as undesirable and irrelevant. In this case, *C* members attempt to effect a complete break with *A* and to establish their own physical and psychological space *not* dictated by *A*. Marcus Garvey's historic back-to-Africa movement, the Black Muslims, and the contemporary black separatists are examples of *C* members in a countercultural withdrawal phase. Independence from white domination for these countercultural members is based on a physical and psychological removal of self from the influence of *A*. This tendency is quite unlike that of members in the aggressive countercultural phase who attempt to free themselves from white domination by effecting change within the white power structure.

It should be noted that this withdrawal phase is frequently, though not necessarily, a result of the failings of the aggressive countercultural phase. Individuals who exerted great effort to effect change in the status quo and failed sometimes retreat into a separatist phase, redefining themselves in terms of their counterculture and relegating the dominant society to irrelevancy. This withdrawal phase, however, is not always a result of the failure of the individual countercultural member to produce a change in the dominant culture. Some, such as Malcolm X, begin in a withdrawal phase and end in an aggressive stage. There are also those whose personalities are such that they never experience an aggressive phase. There are undoubtedly those who, disliking the traditional roles of the white-controlled subculture and not wishing to revolutionize white society, simply immerse themselves in their own racial and ethnic identity. An analogous situation exists now with the many war resisters who recently refused to accept the nation's foreign policy. Some stayed and protested and demonstrated and even went to prison in an aggressive attempt to effect a change; some withdrew entirely and moved to Canada or Sweden or some other country where their views were better accepted.

Communication between countercultural members in the withdrawal phase and members of the dominant culture is minimal or nonexistent. Where such interaction does exist, the *C* member does not normally accept the role expectations held for him by *A;* consequently such interaction is frequently characterized by tension and hostility.

We should remember then that the subcultural role phase is characterized by the racial or ethnic group member's passive acceptance of white domination. In this case, communication with *A* is smooth and tension free as long as the *C* member fulfills the behavioral expectations of the white dominant culture. Subcultural *C* members also have behavioral expectations of *A* members and are made highly uncomfortable by whites who violate those expectations (hippies, revolutionaries, for example). The countercultural aggressive role phase is characterized by aggressive resistance to white domination and dictation of nonwhite behavior and by attempts to change the white-determined status quo. *C* members in the countercultural aggressive phase have definite expectations of white behavior, which include a view of whites as racist and arbitrary. When whites speak and act in a manner at variance with that role expectation, the *C* members are suspicious and distrustful. Finally the countercultural withdrawal phase is characterized by an active withdrawal from the influence of the dominant society. More than any other of the *C* group members, this group is the least concerned with the expectations white society holds of them. By defining whites as irrelevant, they diminish the importance of roles in interracial interaction. In fact, the *C* members of the countercultural withdrawal phase almost psychologically eliminate the necessity of any interracial communication at all. Consequently those members of the white dominant society seeking to engage in and learn from interracial interaction will seldom find any *C* member in the withdrawal phase with whom to communicate.

Ossie Davis, in comparing himself with Malcolm X, delineates and summarizes the philosophical and psychological differences between a "subcultural Negro" and a "contracultural black."

I am a Negro. I am clean, black and I smile a lot. Whenever I want something—to get a job in motion pictures, for instance, or on television or to get a play produced by Broadway, whenever I need a political favor—I go to white folks. White folks have money. I do not. White folks have power. I do not. All of my needs—financial, artistic, social, my need for freedom—I must depend on white folks to supply. That is what is meant by being a Negro.

Malcolm X used to be a Negro, but he stopped. He no longer depended upon white folks to supply his needs—psychologically or sociologically—to give him money or head his fight for freedom or to protect him from enemies or to tell him what to do. Malcolm X did not hate white folks, nor did he love them. Most of all, he did not need them to tell him who he was. Above all, he was determined to make it on his own. That was why Malcolm was no longer a Negro. Malcolm was a man, a black man! A black man means not to accept the system as Negroes do but to fight hell out of the system as Malcolm did. It can be dangerous. Malcolm was killed for it. Nevertheless, I like Malcolm much better than I like myself.[15]

ROLE REVERSAL AND INTERRACIAL COMMUNICATION

Theory and Practice of Role Reversal

Psychologists, psychotherapists, and encounter group leaders are turning more to the technique of role reversal as a means of resolving conflict in interpersonal group communication and as a means of dealing with the kind of interracial role conflict described before. Culbertson defines role reversal as "the taking on of attitudes, feelings, and behaviors that differ from one's own."[16] John

Cohen describes his role-reversal technique as a method whereby two people come to understand their differences when person *A*, if he differs from person *B*, is forced to state *B*'s point of view to the satisfaction of *B*. To present your opponent's point of view accurately, you must truly understand it, and according to Cohen, "by being compelled to genuinely *understand* the opposing viewpoint, each disputant is almost bound to see the situation, at least intellectually, in a new light."[17]

J. L. Moreno, the father of modern psychodrama, expresses a perceptive definition of role reversal:

Role reversal is based on a very ordinary, diurnal idea; how often have we not said in the midst of a heated argument with another person: "But what do you want from me? Just put yourself in my position." Psychodrama is scientific, for it is organized common sense personified. Instead of merely talking about this, we actually do it, by means of role reversal. There is an old American Indian saying which states: "Let me not judge another man until I have walked two weeks in his moccasins."[18]

The practice of role reversal is finding increasing practical application throughout the country in dealing with the mentally disturbed, drug addicts, family counseling, executive training, and race relations. In an experiment at Cedar Knoll in Washington, D.C., a center for mentally disturbed children, psychologists have found that role reversal is extremely helpful in working with patients. "Children, frequently switching roles with the adults, are encouraged to pick out their own strong and weak points and those of other children, and to see themselves as others see them."[19] One disturbed child of 15 said of herself in the exercise: "The bad things about Carolyn. When she gets mad she breaks up a couple of chairs. She curse me out, calls me names."[20] Dr. Jerome Jaffee, head of the Special Action Office for Drug Abuse Prevention, has advocated that every child in the country between the ages of 6 and 16, regardless of social class or racial and ethnic origin, participate in special classes in school in which they engage in role-reversing exercises in order to bring out any latent personality problems that could cause them to turn to drugs later in life.[21] Such exercises are now being employed frequently in education. Teachers Mary Boroughs and Judith Patterson reported on such an activity; they described how they enabled their class to cope with the problem of having a mentally retarded classmate. Marta, an 8-year-old, brain-damaged student, was being ignored by her schoolmates. On a day when Marta was absent, the class participated in a role-reversing exercise in which they portrayed a scene depicting ostracism. So moving was the experience for the 8-year-olds that they made the connection with Marta's plight. After experiencing what she was experiencing, the children began to show her much greater kindness on her return.[22]

"The effort to understand is the beginning of reconciliation," says John Cohen.[23] "The method of role reversal is designed to change the cognitive structure of disputants so that their social perception changes from divergence to convergence."[24] According to Cohen, when a person listens to his position as it is presented by his opponent, he may begin to see it differently and more objectively. He may begin to see some merit in his opponent's objections and reevaluate his own ideas. Conversely when a person attempts to express his opponent's point of view, he may find himself unable to do so accurately and discover that he has been objecting to something he never initially understood. In expressing his opponent's view accurately, he may also find himself somewhat swayed by his own arguments.[25] In testing the effectiveness of role reversal in changing attitudes toward convergence, David W. Johnson experimented to test whether or not "more attitude change will take place when Ss engage in role reversal than when they listen to an opponent role reverse."[26] He found that role reversal is an effective means of changing attitude toward convergence, "that role reversal increases the actor's understanding of the opponent's position."[27] He also found that actively engaging in role reversal has a greater impact on one's change in attitude than does observing someone else reverse a role.

Interracial Role Reversing

A tool as effective as role reversal in overcoming interpersonal conflict and aiding in self-insight appears to be an outstanding method to deal with conflict arising in interracial settings. As stated previously, a major cause of communication breakdown between racial and ethnic groups is a lack of shared experience and an unwillingness to attempt to stand outside of oneself in order to perceive as those with whom one is in conflict may perceive. Role reversal, game that it is, may provide defensive individuals with the structure they need in order to participate in such a necessary empathic experience.

Culbertson,[28] in an experiment dealing with role reversal and racial attitudes, worked on the assumption that attitudes toward minority groups are deeply imbedded, culturally sanctioned, and difficult to change. He asserts that individuals may have to undergo a "therapeutic" experience rather than just an educational process in order to give up "ego-anchored prejudices." His experiment was designed to "unfreeze" the prejudice habit pattern by exploring the effects role reversal has on the attitudes of whites toward blacks. Culbertson hypothesizes that "a role-playing experience involving favorable attitudes toward integration of Negro and white housing results in a favorable modification of the pertinent specific attitude, and to a lesser degree, in a more favorable generalized attitude toward the Negro."[29] In the experimental role-reversal exercise individuals against integrated housing were assigned the task of speaking in favor of it in a group discussion. The results of the experiment verified the hypothesis; the subjects shifted their attitudes toward black–white integration in housing as well as their general attitude toward blacks.[30]

Such interracial role-reversing experiments are being conducted not only in the isolation of the social science laboratory but also in real-life situations where racial tension interferes with group productivity. At United States Marine Camp Lejeune, for example, race relations have been marred by a long history of tension and violence. A marine corporal was beaten to death over a racial dispute, and brawls and assaults caused by interracial friction were commonplace. In order to reverse this dangerous and wasteful trend, camp officials introduced a concentrated program to "open communication across racial lines." Role-reversing exercises were carried out in which white sergeants played the role of black militants and black enlisted men presented their perception of their white superior officers. The following is an example of the dialogue produced when white officers reversed roles with blacks:

Just because my skin is black, I get all the garbage details. Why does it happen only to the Brothers [blacks] and never to the Chuck Dudes [whites]? When you talk to a Chuck [white], you say, "Would you please," and when you talk to a black man you just say, "Do it." And your tone of voice shows me you're saying, "You're black and I'm going to get over on you."[31]

The black enlisted men presented their view of the white officer as follows:

"I've tried to counsel these people—I can't do anything with them."
"You have two choices; either you do it, like I say, or go to jail."[32]

Those who participated in this exercise felt that the experience forced them to see through the eyes of their opponents. A white sergeant expressed his reaction to the role-reversal experience:

"Everything seems so one-sided. The officers seemed to have their minds made up; I always got the feeling I was being railroaded and they gave me no chance to communicate at all."[33]

This kind of insight into the interracial dilemma, this ability to see for the first time "how the other guy feels," resulted in a dramatic reduction of interracial hostility and violence at Camp Lejeune.

One of the most dramatic experiments in role reversal that has come to the attention of the public is that conducted by Mrs. Jane Elliot, a third-grade school teacher at the Community Elementary School in Riceville, Iowa. The experience of her class was popularized in an ABC documentary in 1971 entitled "Eye of the Storm." In her town, with a population of 898, Mrs. Elliot observed that there were no black inhabitants, that all the townspeople were Christians, and that the textbooks in the school represented this limited view of the population. She found that the children in her school had attitudes that reflected the ignorance and prejudice of their homes; the students viewed blacks in the abstract as dirty, smelly, violent, and dumb. When Martin Luther King, Jr., was assassinated, Mrs. Elliot decided it was time that her students learned what racial discrimination really meant.

She called for a two-day exercise that she entitled "Discrimination Day." Her class was divided into two groups based on eye color. On the first day the brown-eyed children were arbitrarily picked as superior and were given many privileges denied to the blue-eyed children. They were allowed water fountain privileges, were granted longer recesses, were given the opportunity to be first in the lunch line and to enjoy seconds, were given seats in the front of the class, had better playground facilities, and, in general, were given positive reinforcement. The blue-eyed children were denied all these privileges and given negative reinforcement. On the second day of the exercise, the roles were reversed; the blue-eyed children became the privileged group, and the brown-eyed children now occupied second-rate positions in the class. Mrs. Elliot describes the amazing results of the first day's experience in arbitrary discrimination:

By lunch hour, there was no need to think before identifying a child as blue- or brown-eyed. I could tell simply by looking at them. The brown-eyed children were happy, alert, having the time of their lives. And they were doing far better work than they had ever done before. The blue-eyed children were miserable. Their postures, their expressions, their entire attitudes were those of defeat. Their classroom work regressed sharply from that of the day before. Inside of an hour or so, they looked and acted as though they were, in fact, inferior. It was shocking.

But even more frightening was the way the brown-eyed children turned on their friends of the day before, the way they accepted almost immediately as true what had originally been described as an exercise. For there was no question, after an hour or so, that they actually believed they were superior.[34]

When the roles were reversed, the blue-eyed children became happy and the brown-eyed children became despondent, nervous, and resentful. The only difference in the reaction of the children on the second day of the exercise was that the blue-eyed children, having experienced discrimination the day before, were less cruel to the brown-eyed students than the latter had been when they were in the positions of superiority.

The reactions of the children to this experience were quite dramatic. Brown-eyed Debbie Anderson said:

"I felt mad and I wanted to tie the people with blue eyes up and quit school because they got to do everything first and we had to do everything last. I felt dirty and I did not feel as smart as I did on Friday. Discrimination is no fun."[35]

Blue-eyed Theodore Perzynski stated his reaction as follows:

"I felt like slapping a brown-eyed person. It made me mad. Then I felt like kicking a brown-eyed person. I felt like quitting school. I do not like discrimination. It makes me sad. I would not like to be angry all my life."[36]

The reactions of the children were thus emotional in the extreme: "I felt dirty," "I was sick," "I didn't feel like I was very big," "I felt like quitting school," "I felt like crying," "I felt left out," "I felt like kicking a brown-eyed person," "I felt like being a dropout."[37]

Mrs. Elliot was thus able to simulate the experiences of nonwhite groups in this country with amazing accuracy. The resentment, hostility, insecurity, apathy, and depression her children experienced after only one day of being subjected to arbitrary discriminatory behavior provided an extraordinary microcosm of the effects of prolonged and institutionally sanctioned discrimination. Her children learned through actually experiencing discrimination what they never could have grasped in a conventional educational structure. The role reversal provided them with a profound communicative experience in which they developed an aptitude for empathy which will undoubtedly have great impact on their lives.

Role-reversing exercises can also provide adults with insightful experiences, particularly in an interracial group. By watching others portray us, we are frequently enlightened regarding how they perceive us. The author conducted a series of role-reversing exercises within an ongoing interracial group of university students; some interesting hypotheses were derived concerning interracial understanding and role relationships.

The group was composed of white, black, and chicano students. In the first portion of the role activity, the blacks in the group formed a subgroup and engaged in a discussion in front of the remainder of the group members. In this discussion they presented their concept of a group of white community residents discussing the notion of busing to achieve racial integration in the public schools. Portrayed by the blacks were a "police" type who objected to busing and felt that the infiltration of blacks into a white neighborhood would make the area unsafe, a "politician" who was constantly searching for expedient answers that would lose him the least number of votes, a "banker" type whose entire concern was the gain or loss of revenue the program would entail, a "social worker" type who spoke up vehemently for busing but admitted that her children would not be affected by it because they were enrolled in private schools, and a "white radical" type who hurled attacks at the establishment but admitted he had never done anything to better the conditions in his own community. The entire rendition was designed to reveal to the white students the black perceptions of white monetary fixations and white hypocrisy regarding racial integration. The white students expressed surprise at the accuracy with which the blacks had portrayed such pervasive white attitudes and were anxious to present their concept of black behavior.

A rather dramatic occurrence resulted from the white attempt to portray black discussants. After three minutes of delivering cliché stereotypic statements, the white students found themselves unable to proceed. They stated they did not have the words to express black feelings as blacks would express them, because they had never really listened to the manner in which blacks expressed themselves. This provided insight for the white participants; they realized that to them blacks had indeed been "invisible" men.

All discussants offered interesting hypotheses regarding the causes of this phenomenon, the blacks' ability to portray whites with such precision and the whites' inability to portray blacks. Whites for the most part, having been in control of the dominant culture, have not previously been concerned with fulfilling the role expectations of blacks; they have not consistently had to take the role of blacks to determine black expectations in order to survive. Consequently they have been aware of black behavior only in the most stereotypic fashion as it has been projected to them through the media and through the playing-at-a-role behavior of the blacks themselves. Such a superficial exposure had resulted in basic ignorance on the part of whites regarding black attitudes and beliefs. For these reasons, the discussants hypothesized, whites were unable to portray blacks in a sociodramatic setting.

Blacks, on the other hand, as exemplified in *The Spook Who Sat by the Door,* constantly have had to take the role of whites and determine white expectations to survive. In integrated situations, for self-preservation, they have had to master white attitudes. Consequently, when called upon to reverse roles, they accomplish their portrayals with great facility.

A final exercise was conducted by the group in which the chicanos attempted to portray whites and blacks. They were unable to play either. Despite the variable of individual abilities in role reversing, this phenomenon also suggested an interesting hypothesis. The chicanos themselves felt that blacks and whites were more alike and had a greater shared understanding of values than the chicanos had of either blacks or whites. The chicanos considered themselves more of a subculture, removed from the dominant culture by strong custom, tradition, and language. The blacks, on the other hand, were regarded as a counterculture, an outgrowth of and a reaction to the larger society and consequently closer to the white society with regard to values and custom. In terms of the interracial model presented in Chapter 1, the chicanos felt they related more to circle *B* than to *C* or *A* and that blacks, having been denied a *B* circle, were firmly entrenched in circle *C* and were more greatly compelled to relate to circle *A* for survival.

Whereas these generalizations apply only to the behavior of this particular interracial unit, and are speculative at best, they do provide some interesting considerations for future research in interracial interaction.

THE FUTURE

The role revolution in contemporary society is far-reaching and crucial to any form of interpersonal communication, whether interracial, interethnic, or intersexual. Chicanos, American Indians, blacks, Japanese, Chinese, Filipinos, Puerto Ricans, and many others are refusing to accept the roles imposed on them by the general society and are forming new behavioral expectations for themselves. Women are awakening to the call of liberation as well and are rejecting the traditional roles of cook, housekeeper, and babysitter. Because we are now in a dramatic state of flux as the old roles are being replaced with new ones, communication between individuals who do not agree on role expectations has become increasingly difficult and unstable. Interracial and interethnic communication will become predictable only when these new roles are fully defined so that all participating communicators share relatively the same understanding of behavioral expectations. Until that time, interracial and interethnic communication will be volatile and, at times, self-destructive, as individuals search in the midst of chaos to discover and digest a new pattern of role behavior.

Activities

1. Name at least five roles you commonly play. What are the behavioral expectations accompanying those roles? Do they ever conflict?
2. Describe some of your experiences with role taking. Why do you do it? Do you ever play at a role? For what purpose?
3. Have you ever rejected the behavioral obligations of a role as-

signed to you? When and why? Do you see yourself as fitting into any of the role phases described in this chapter? Which ones? How does this affect your participation in interracial communication situations?

4. Divide the class into racial groups and conduct a role-reversing exercise. Each racial group must portray the behavior they think typical of another racial group in any situation they wish to create. For example, a group of black students might wish to portray their concept of the behavior of an all-white PTA meeting dealing with the subject of busing. After each role rendition conduct an open class discussion enabling the group portrayed to respond to what they have just witnessed. Remember that the essential point of this exercise is not to reveal how we really are but how others see us.

5. Read *The Spook Who Sat by the Door* by Sam Greenlee (New York: Bantam, 1970) and write a detailed analysis of the role playing, role taking, playing at a role, and role conflict of the various characters. To what degree do you feel this book accurately reflects the role relationships between blacks and whites in our society? Why?

NOTES

1. Cf. Erving Goffman, *The Presentation of Self in Everyday Life* (Garden City, N.Y.: Doubleday, 1959).
2. Ralph H. Turner, "Role-Taking, Role Standpoint, and Reference Group Behavior," in Edward E. Sampson, *Approaches, Contexts, and Problems of Social Psychology* (Englewood Cliffs, N.J.: Prentice-Hall, 1965), p. 219.
3. Robert Redfield, *The Folk Culture of Yucatán* (Chicago: The University of Chicago Press, 1941), p. 132.
4. Tamotsu Shibutani, *Society and Personality* (Englewood Cliffs, N.J.: Prentice-Hall, 1961), p. 40.
5. Ibid., p. 60.
6. Ibid., p. 56.
7. J. Milton Yinger, "Contraculture and Subculture," in Sampson, op. cit., p. 465.
8. Ibid.
9. Shibutani, op. cit., pp. 575–576.
10. Sam Greenlee, *The Spook Who Sat by the Door* (New York: Bantam, 1970), pp. 4–5.

11. Yinger, op. cit., p. 468.
12. Ibid.
13. William Thomas and Florian Znaniecki, *The Polish Peasant in Europe and America,* vol. II (New York: Knopf, 1927), pp. 1117–1264, 1303–1306, 1647–1827.
14. Andrea L. Rich, "Dissemblance in Communicative Response," *Western Speech* (Winter 1971): 42–47.
15. Lerone Bennett, Jr., "What's in a Name?" *EBONY Magazine* (November, 1967). Reprinted by permission of *EBONY Magazine.* Copyright 1967 by Johnson Publishing Company, Inc.
16. Frances M. Culbertson, "Modification of an Emotionally Held Attitude Through Role Playing," *J. Abnor. Psychol.* 54 (1957): 23.
17. John Cohen, "The Technique of Role Reversal: A Preliminary Note," *Occup. Psychol.* 25 (1957): 64–65.
18. J. L. Moreno, ed., *The International Handbook of Psychotherapy* (New York: Philosophical Library, 1966), p. 240.
19. Phillip A. McCombs, "Cedar Knoll Psychodrama," *The Washington Post,* 6 May 1971.
20. Ibid.
21. Arnold A. Hutshnecker, "A Plan for Preventing Abuse of Drugs," *The New York Times,* 22 March 1972.
22. Mary Boroughs and Judith Patterson, "Marta Joins the Class," *Grade Teacher* 15 (1964): 74–75.
23. Cohen, op. cit., p. 65.
24. Ibid.
25. Ibid., p. 64.
26. David W. Johnson, "Effectiveness of Role Reversal: Actor or Listener," *Psychol. Rep.* 28 (1971): 279.
27. Ibid., p. 282.
28. Culbertson, op. cit., p. 231.
29. Ibid.
30. Ibid., p. 232.
31. Thomas Johnson, "Marines Easing Racial Tensions and Violence at Camp Lejeune," *The New York Times,* 21 January 1971.
32. Ibid.
33. Ibid.
34. William Peters, *A Class Divided* (Garden City, N.Y.: Doubleday, 1971), pp. 24–25.
35. Ibid., p. 33.
36. Ibid.
37. Ibid., p. 35.

5

Beliefs, Attitudes, Values, and Interracial Communication

At the core of our previous discussions regarding perception, stereotyping, culture, roles, and interracial communication is the assumption that each individual has specific cognitions regarding the existence or nonexistence of certain objects and/or states of being. Such cognitions are commonly referred to as "beliefs." Individuals also bring with them to the interracial communication situation predispositions to favor or disfavor such objects or states. These predispositions compose the communicator's "attitudes." Finally individuals also possess various notions concerning appropriate and desirable ways of behaving with regard to the environment; such concepts of appropriateness constitute the communicator's "value" orientation.

We are cognitively and emotionally bound by notions of what is true and false, good and bad, desirable and undesirable, appropriate and inappropriate. The concepts of "belief," "attitude," and "value" are crucial to the understanding of the dynamics of interracial communication, because they frequently dictate and structure overt behavior.

BELIEFS AND INTERRACIAL COMMUNICATION

Definition
A belief is the apprehension of the existence of something. It answers the question, "Is an object or state of being real?" Related to the "probability dimension" of a concept, belief deals with probable or improbable existence.[1] Belief is related to perception, for it involves the perception of the existence of a relationship: "If a man perceives a relationship between two things, or between something and a characteristic of it, he is said to hold a belief."[2]

We act on the basis of what we expect is true or what we expect exists. If we believe a stove is hot, we avoid placing an unprotected hand on it. If we believe a snake is poisonous, we attempt to maintain a safe distance from it. Belief therefore deals with what we expect from our environment, or as Rokeach states: "Beliefs are inferences made by an observer about underlying states of expectancy."[3]

Because belief is composed of a personal perception, the content of a belief cannot be directly observed by others but must be inferred by an observer on the basis of the overt behavior of the believer. That which the believer says or does becomes the clue to his belief system. A child, for example, attempting to be brave, may say he is not afraid of dogs. Yet when he runs to the other side of the street on seeing a dog approach him, his action reveals more about his belief regarding the quality of dogs than does his overt statement of belief. In this case we infer the boy's belief on the basis of his action.

Likewise a white man who publicly states that he believes blacks are equal to him but who resists blacks moving into his neighborhood expresses more about his belief system through his actions than through his conscious statement of belief. Thus in order to discern a person's perception of reality, we must infer his belief patterns through the observation of all he says and does. Because we frequently assume that belief precedes action, we might conclude, on seeing a man avoiding a stove, that he believes the stove is hot. In the social realm, as we perceive a member of one race consistently avoiding members of another race, we will likely infer the existence of a belief of superiority, inferiority, or even fear.

Belief, then, constitutes an individual's concept of reality. We detect the existence of a particular belief only through inference based on the observation of an individual's behavior and on the assumption that that behavior is guided by belief.

A Classification of Beliefs

A system for the classification of beliefs, such as that developed by Milton Rokeach,[4] is relevant to the understanding of belief as it functions as part of the interracial communication structure. Rokeach's classification is based on the assumption that an individual's beliefs are not all equally important, but vary in intensity, with the most central beliefs the more resistant to change and having a greater impact on the belief system if they are changed.

Rokeach offers five types of belief, which he labels type *A* to type *E* and which proceed from *A* (the most central) to *E* (the most peripheral). Type *A* beliefs are primitive beliefs that require 100 percent consensus. They relate to sense perceptions such as concepts of color, size, shape, sound, and space. They are learned through an individual's direct encounter with his environment. For example, everyone agrees fire is hot and snow is cold. Type *B* beliefs are also primitive but require no consensus; that is, one need not receive outside verification from other sources to maintain this belief. For example, one believes in the existence of his own pain, grief, sorrow, or suffering even if others deny the existence of such feelings. Like type *A* beliefs, *B* beliefs are based on an individual's personal experience with his environment. If, for example, a chicano in Texas has experienced racist treatment all his life, he might believe that America is a racist country, and a national declaration claiming the nonexistence of racism would not change his primitive type *B* belief. Primitive beliefs, types *A* and *B*, constitute the core of an individual's belief system. They are psychologically incontrovertible and have a taken-for-granted character. These beliefs encompass the individual's notion of "basic truth" about the physical world, the social world, and the world of self. For example, beliefs such as "the world is round," "he is my father," and "I am white" constitute central beliefs and are enormously resistant to change.

Types *C* and *D* beliefs, beliefs based on authoritative sources and reference groups, are less central and hence are more susceptible to change than types *A* and *B*. The Bible may serve as a source of authority for me, the Koran for you. Mr. X may put his entire trust in *The New York Times,* whereas Mr. Y may only read *The Daily News.* George McGovern may have been your man for the Presidency and Richard Nixon mine. These authority beliefs and derived beliefs are important in determining a person's actions, but they are open to change.

Finally, type *E* beliefs, or inconsequential beliefs, are primarily matters of personal taste and are not dependent on social opinion. They are more personal and arbitrary and require no consensus.

Such beliefs are derived from a person's direct exposure to the object of belief; for example, "pears are more delicious than peaches." An inconsequential belief is also quite resistant to change but, being peripheral, does not much affect the more central aspects of a person's belief system.

Belief Conflict in Interracial Communication

Conflict arising from differences in primitive beliefs among communicators is one of the major sources of disruption in interracial communication. Primitive beliefs based on an individual's direct personal experience with reality are held firmly, even dearly, and are stubbornly resistant to change. In Chapter 1 the diagram depicting the interracial communication environment suggested that A (members of the white dominant power structure) and C (members of the nonwhite community) actually *experience* a different reality. Such a divergence in experience will consequently result in a different set of primitive or core beliefs. Understanding this variation in primitive beliefs between members of different racial and ethnic groups points to the enormous distance between interracial communicators and the problems they must overcome in order to engage in productive interaction.

A Swedish immigrant to the United States might be heard to say: "I came penniless to America twenty-five years ago, and I now have a business from which I earn $30,000 per year. America is indeed a land of opportunity, even for a foreigner of humble background like me." A chicano immigrant to the San Joaquin Valley of California, on the other hand, might say: "I came penniless to America twenty-five years ago and have worked long back-breaking hours as a migrant fruit picker ever since. I live in shacks and tents with my frequently hungry family. America is surely a land of oppression for the poor worker." These two individuals, in adjusting to America, actually experienced different realities. Consequently each holds a different belief regarding the American reality. Each belief is true for each individual, and each belief, based on direct experience, is incontrovertible.

Fred L. Hartley, president of Union Oil Company, recently responded to an assertion regarding the existence of people in America who subsist on the starvation level by stating: "I don't believe it. You don't believe it either . . . You bring me 10 people in this room right now who need food and I'll give it to them. You can't do it. It is impossible . . . I don't believe it. When people starve, they get violent. And we haven't had any food riots since I was a boy."[5] Further, when asked, "Have you ever gone hungry in your life?" he responded: "When I was raised, I never had a period in my life when I didn't know where my next meal was coming from." Insensitive as his statements might appear to those who today do not know where their next meal is coming from, Mr. Hartley is merely expressing his primitive beliefs based on his own personal experience. As president of one of the world's largest corporations, it is not likely that hunger is a problem to him now; by his own admission it has never constituted a major obstacle in his life.

If we compare Mr. Hartley's description of his early experience or nonexperience with hunger with that described by Richard Wright in his autobiographical *Black Boy,*[6] we can see the development of an interracial conflict in primitive beliefs. Wright vividly describes how as a child he would fill his stomach with water to ward off the pain of hunger, his constant childhood companion. Had Mr. Hartley and Mr. Wright ever met and engaged in an interracial interaction, there undoubtedly would have arisen a conflict in primitive beliefs based on the extreme disparity between the personal experience and perception of reality of each. A white middle-class engineer and a nonwhite high school dropout might encounter the same primitive belief conflict. For the engineer, school provided a career and the opportunity to succeed economically. Consequently he most probably would believe that the school system is fine. The dropout, on the other hand, might have experienced a constant negative reinforcement in school. Perhaps the institution discriminated against him because he was bilingual, or perhaps the skills it taught and emphasized did not seem to relate directly to his life and needs. For such a youth, the school system is a source of pain and failure. Again, different life experiences result in different primitive beliefs and lead toward conflict when individuals of diverse backgrounds interact.

To overcome the obstacle of conflict in primitive belief systems inherent in most interracial communication, the communicators must accomplish a difficult task: They must acknowledge the possibility of the existence of a reality other than their own, a reality that they may never have experienced personally. Communicators must also develop the attitude of *wanting* to learn about the reality of others. We possess an eager attitude and curiosity when we interact with people in different countries; yet we refuse to do the same with members of other racial and ethnic groups in our own country. This desire to learn and understand the realities of others must be reciprocal in an interracial setting. Only when communicators are willing to take the giant step toward the acknowledgment of multiple realities will they be able to overcome conflicts in primitive beliefs.

The more peripheral beliefs in a belief system can also come into conflict in the interracial communication situation. Different races have different authority figures whom they regard as credible. Angela Davis is a heroine to some young blacks and a dangerous subversive to some white middle-class Americans. George Wallace is likewise a mentor and promise for the future to some elements of the population (primarily white working class) and is viewed as a Hitlerian figure by others. The Berrigan brothers and Daniel Ellsberg may be heroes to the peace movement but traitors to American hawks.

Although divergent views regarding authority beliefs can be very disruptive in interracial communication, it should be remembered that types *C* and *D* beliefs are controvertible; that is, people do change opinions regarding authority figures. Malcolm X, for example, was first viewed by whites as a dangerous revolutionary but has now achieved a more "respectable" status in the eyes of the white population when compared with the Black Panther revolutionary movement. Based on the same value system, the passive-resistance methods of Martin Luther King have made him almost saintlike when compared with the Panther doctrine of armed self-defense. A look at the political arena also demonstrates that authority beliefs do change. The late President Lyndon Johnson, for example, winning in 1964 in a landslide victory, felt such a change in public sentiment that he did not choose to run for reelection. Political front-runners may decline quickly and underdogs may make stellar rises in public opinion polls.

In an interracial communication situation, evidence is relevant to changing nonprimitive beliefs. Such change, however, is particularly difficult if the believer in authority is unyielding and cannot be induced to listen to issues worthy of the test of evidence and subject to probative force. If, for example, a person believes in George Wallace totally on the basis of charisma and not on the basis of the issues for which he stands, then that belief becomes almost a type *E* belief in that it is based upon personal taste and hence is incontrovertible.

Many authority beliefs are issue-related. For example, a Wallace supporter, defending his position, may state: "I like George Wallace because: (1) He's for the workingman; (2) he's against busing." These issues now become open for dispute, discussion, and evidence. Persuasive communication between members of different races holding different beliefs about Wallace can proceed. The resulting communication may be extremely argumentative in nature; nevertheless, the issues are open for discussion. In order to engage in interracial communication regarding a conflict in authority-based beliefs, then, communicators must be able to reduce such beliefs to concrete statements of issues and to bring evidence to bear on those issues.

Whereas discussion regarding a conflict in types *C* and *D* beliefs can proceed productively in the interracial arena, type *E* beliefs do not lend themselves to fruitful interracial communication. Discussion on matters of personal taste, on the charismatic appeal of leaders, the taste of good food, the pleasant sound of music, and other value-laden beliefs is seldom successful in changing opinions. It should be remembered that many type *E* beliefs are also culturally determined. What is beautiful depends on the standards of beauty of the culture. "Black is beautiful" is a reaction to a culture that has long defined beauty in terms of white features only. If Harry Belafonte is attractive to whites, it is because, as Archie Bunker says, "He's really a white guy dipped in caramel." That is to say, he is still being judged by white standards of beauty. An interracial discussion regarding respective cultural tastes can be highly informative, in much the same way we study standards of art and beauty of other countries. An argument, however, of the relative merit of a particular type *E* belief, that black is prettier than white or Spanish more beautiful and expressive than English, is counterproductive and might lead to hostility rather than mutual respect and understanding. Just as in the case of a conflict in primitive beliefs in which we must acknowledge multiple realities, when dealing with a conflict in type *E* beliefs, we must acknowledge multiple standards of personal taste.

Belief then as the individual's concept of reality is a crucial element in an interracial encounter. Given the different racial and ethnic realities of the United States, conflict in beliefs on all levels serves as a persistent obstacle to interracial communication.

Such an obstacle can be overcome only through the acknowledgment of multiple realities and standards by all interracial interaction participants.

ATTITUDES AND INTERRACIAL COMMUNICATION

Definition

Belief is not the only communicator attribute that profoundly affects the outcome of interracial communication; an individual's *attitudes* play an equally important role in the interracial communication situation. Attitudes are more complex than beliefs, for they add to individual beliefs an affective or feeling state regarding the objects of belief. As Bem suggests: "Attitudes are likes and dislikes. They are our affinity for and our aversion to situations, objects, persons, groups, or any other identifiable aspects of our environment, including abstract ideas and social policies."[7]

This "affinity for and aversion to" objects and situations in the environment also constitutes a set of predispositions that guide an individual's behavior toward the object of his attitude. "Attitudes have generally been regarded as either mental readinesses or implicit predispositions which exert some general and consistent influence on a fairly large class of evaluative responses. These responses are usually directed toward some object, person, or group."[8] Attitudes guide the communicator's response patterns so as to make it impossible for him to react in a neutral fashion; they force him to act in a selective manner toward certain specific stimulus situations. "Attitudes create a functional state of readiness which determines the organism to react in a characteristic way."[9] Further, attitudes are relatively enduring predispositions that are not innate but are learned experientially. Although they are not momentarily transient, they are susceptible to change through the individual's experience in new situations.[10]

Attitudes and Belief

Attitudes and beliefs are interconnected; according to Rokeach, attitudes actually consist of a "package of beliefs . . . a relatively enduring organization of beliefs around an object or situation predisposing one to respond in some preferential manner."[11] Katz also views attitudes as consisting of a belief plus some affective state: "Attitudes include both the affective or feeling core of liking or disliking, and the cognitive or belief element which describes the object of the attitude, its characteristics, its relation to other objects. All attitudes thus include beliefs, but not all beliefs are attitudes."[12] An example might help to clarify the relationship between attitude and belief. The following statement consists of only a belief: "Blacks invented soul music." This statement asserts the existence of a relationship between soul music and the black race. It makes no statement regarding the believer's feelings toward or evaluation of either soul music or the black race. The statement, "I like black soul music," is an attitudinal statement; that is, it includes a belief ("black soul music" is equated with "soul music is black") plus the affective assertion that the believer likes the object of belief and is hence favorably disposed to it. An attitude thus consists of a belief and an evaluation of that belief: "X is a communist" (belief), and "I don't like X" (attitude).

Acquisition, Detection, and Communication of Attitudes

"Attitudes are acquired out of social experience and provide the individual organism with some degree of preparation to adjust in a well defined way to certain types of social situations, if and when these situations arise."[13] In interracial situations one is not born hostile. He learns through personal experience (firsthand or secondhand through the experience of relevant others) that some individuals in racial and ethnic groups have embraced him and others have rejected him. In response to such differential treatment, he feels comfortable and has approach predispositions or attitudes toward those friendly to him; conversely he experiences discomfort, avoidance predispositions, and hostile attitudes toward those who he feels have rejected him. Attitudes thus develop in the same fashion as do stereotypes through our own experience, the experience of those whom we love and admire, and exposure to the communication media of the society. Racist images that the media—books, magazines, newspapers, motion pictures, radio, and television—project (discussed in the chapter on stereotypes) likewise determine pervasive racist attitudes held by the members of society exposed to such communications. In the interracial setting all communicators bring these predispositions to the communication act. As many have recently experienced, interracial interaction is frequently characterized more by avoidance responses and hostility than by approach predispositions. For interracial communication to proceed at all, however, it is necessary for some degree of approach response to exist purely on pragmatic grounds. If the avoidance predisposition becomes stronger than the need to engage in interracial interaction, individuals will not choose to come together in an interracial setting, and no communication can ensue.

Attitudes are as difficult to detect as beliefs, because, like beliefs, they can only be *inferred* from verbal and nonverbal reactions of individuals. When a communicator repeatedly reacts positively or negatively in relation to a certain stimulus object, we infer that he has established a specific attitude.[14] By observing carefully how an individual responds to certain objects in his environment, we infer that "the object of attitude is placed in a category or class favorable or unfavorable in some degree, high or low in some degree in the individual's scheme of things."[15] The behavior we observe to detect an individual's attitude is the vehicle for the communication of attitudes. The most reliable behavior in terms of accurately predicting attitudes is physical reflex responses. These responses are incapable of being controlled by the communicator; hence, even if the communicator wanted to express an attitude overtly, his reflex responses might give the lie to his verbal expression. The lyric, "your lips tell me 'No No,' but there's 'Yes Yes' in your eyes," is a corny yet accurate reminder that physical behavior (facial expression, body movement, posture) is the most accurate indication of attitudes. When we like something or want something, we tend to pull ourselves closer to it, to approach it, and hence communicate a positive attitude to it. When we dislike something, we pull away, sometimes so subtly as to be almost imperceptible; nevertheless, we demonstrate an avoidance response and a negative attitude. Various physical acts that communicate attitudes will be discussed more fully in the chapter on nonverbal communication. Meanwhile, it should be remembered that most tension and hostility in interracial communication is based on the attitudes of the communicators and the verbal and nonverbal manner in which those attitudes are expressed and interpreted.

Prejudice: A Pervasive Interracial Attitude

One of the most all-encompassing and disruptive attitudes consistently surfacing in interracial interaction is racial prejudice. This attitude was discussed in some depth in Chapter 2, in terms of its definition, its origin, and its effects of interracial perception and communication. A discussion of prejudice is included briefly in this chapter only to identify it as an *attitude*. Prejudice as an attitude dictates a communicator's predisposition to respond in a particular manner, in this case, with a negative or avoidance response. Like all attitudes prejudice is composed of a belief *and* an evaluation of that belief:

attitude of racial prejudice =

belief: another person is racially distinct from self

+

evaluation: a dislike of that distinction (negative feeling toward those who are racially different)

An in-depth discussion of the beliefs, attitudes, and values that are particularly disruptive to interracial encounters will be included later in this chapter.

Object Attitude and Situation Attitude

The stimuli or objects in the environment toward which we hold certain attitudes do not exist in isolation; rather, we normally perceive such objects within the context of some social situation. How a person reacts to an *object within a situation* depends on his predispositional beliefs regarding the object *and* his predispositional beliefs regarding the situation. According to Rokeach a person's behavior must always be mediated by at least two types of attitudes, one activated by the object and the other activated by the situation.[16]

Our behavior toward a Mexican, for example, is dictated both by our attitude toward the Mexican as an object and our attitude toward the situation in which we find him. One responds differently toward the Mexican in Mexico and the Mexican who is regarded as a foreigner in the United States. How a white person responds to a black man swimming in a previously segregated swimming pool includes both attitudes about blacks and about poolside settings. Thus whereas objects and situations interact, one may dominate the other. If a white objects to the presence of the black, it is probably based on his attitude toward the situation: He may respond positively to the same black man digging a ditch or cleaning a house. He is therefore responding to the *object within a situation* rather than the object alone and unrelated to his environment.

Attitudes and Interracial Communication

The difference between object and situational attitudes is revealed in studies of attitudes expressed in face-to-face interracial encounters as opposed to those expressed in impersonal interracial contacts. In non-face-to-face settings, people feel freer to express discriminatory attitudes toward the objects (in this case the Chinese), whereas their attitudes toward propriety of behavior in an interracial situation inhibited them from expressing these same sentiments in face-to-face encounters. Richard La Piere[17] conducted a study in which he traveled for two years with a Chinese student and his wife. During that time only one hotel refused them accommodations. Six months later, La Piere sent follow-up questionnaires to the same hotels that had previously accepted the Chinese couple and asked if they would accept Chinese guests; 92 percent of the hotels replied "No." Again we see the tendency to express one racial attitude in a face-to-face interracial setting and a contrary one in an impersonal situation. The situation has dictated the behavior.

Kutner and others[18] conducted a similar study. Like La Piere, they wanted to find the reason for the discrepancy between behavior supposedly dependent on the same constellation of attitudes. Two white women entered a restaurant and asked for a table for three, explaining that the third party would arrive shortly. After they were seated, a black woman entered, told the hostess that her party was already seated, and joined the two white women. All three ladies received excellent service. The incident was repeated a number of times. Two weeks later each restaurant received a letter requesting a dinner party reservation for a black group. The restaurants did not respond to the letters. The experimenters also telephoned the same restaurants requesting reservations for a black group. The restaurants, in the more personal phone contact, avoided saying "No" but tried to dissuade the callers by stating that they took no reservations. This study revealed that the more the direct contact, the less likely the restaurants were to engage in overt discrimination. The less personal the contact, the more likely the establishment was to discriminate on a racial basis.

These studies point to an incongruity between peoples' personally held and publicly expressed attitudes. The pressures of decorum in a face-to-face interracial situation seem to inhibit the overt expression of prejudice. This tendency may explain the black stereotype of whites as "evasive" and "concealing," as suggested in Chapter 3. The dissemblance response displayed in public interracial settings tends to verify the lack of trust many nonwhites have for whites.

Expression of interracial attitudes becomes more important on the more interpersonal level of interracial contact. The previous studies dealt with only the most superficial type of interaction. Attitudes have their deepest impact on interaction in interracial social, discussion, and work groups. In these situations two types of attitudes relevant to interracial communication are held: (1) the attitudes that communicators have toward each other and (2) the attitudes that they possess regarding objects and situations in the environment beyond their immediate selves and group, for example, social issues or political positions.

The first type of attitude deals with those predispositions communicators have toward members of other racial or ethnic groups in face-to-face settings. Although public decorum may demand a pleasant verbal or nonverbal exchange, attitudes expressed nonverbally are the true indicators. As the group moves away from the public environment, the pressures to mask the expression of true attitudes diminishes, and interracial avoidance patterns can be detected more easily because they are expressed more openly. Facial expressions (glares of resentment, boredom, dismissal, distrust, mockery, condescension, arrogance) and physical postures (tension, retraction, attempts to maintain physical isolation, attempts to make physical contact such as handshaking, touching, or patting) reveal a multitude of attitudes in the interracial setting. Such actions may constitute a clear communication of an attitude, particularly when the physical expression and the verbal expression are mutually consistent or the communication of interracial attitudes is ambiguous. A threatening fist raised by a hostile angry nonwhite may be a clear statement of his attitude at that moment, whereas the gentle pat by a white liberal may be considerably more ambiguous. Such a gesture as the latter could suggest a friendship-seeking approach response or one of condescension, or it could constitute a personal attempt to overcome the fear of interracial contact by engaging overtly in that contact, similar to the impulse to dive rapidly into a cold lake. There does seem to exist, in the interracial communication situation, a "touch–don't touch" compulsion. Many individuals feel compelled to make physical contact with members of another race in order to express an approach attitude. Sometimes this physical movement accurately expresses a communicator's attitude, and sometimes it functions as a convoluted way of trying to avoid betraying an actual avoidance response toward members of another race. How nonverbal expressions of attitude affect interracial communication will be discussed in greater depth in the chapter on nonverbal communication. How differences in attitudes toward objects (excluding attitudes communicators have toward each other) affect interracial communication and interpersonal attraction will be discussed later in this chapter.

VALUES AND INTERRACIAL COMMUNICATION

Definition
Like beliefs and attitudes, values are influential in dictating the behavior of a communicator in interracial settings. According to Rokeach, a value is a type of belief, centrally located within one's total belief system, that deals with the manner in which someone ought or ought not to behave or about some end-state of existence worth or not worth attaining.[19] Values are thus abstract ideals; they may be consciously conceived or unconsciously held and, like beliefs and attitudes, must be inferred from what a person says or does. "A person's value system may thus be said to represent a learned organization of rules for making choices and for resolving conflicts, between two or more modes of behavior or between two or more end-states of existence."[20] Kluckhohn agrees with this definition: "A value is a conception, explicit or distinctive of an individual or characteristic of a group, of the desirable which influences the selection from available modes, means, and ends of action."[21]

Values, then, tell us how we should behave. They can further be classified as instrumental or terminal. Bem suggests the distinction between instrumental and terminal values in his definition of the concept of value: "Value is a primitive preference for or a positive attitude toward certain end-states of existence (like equality, salvation, self-fulfillment, or freedom), or certain broad modes of conduct (like courage, honesty, friendship, or chastity)."[22] An instrumental value deals with a preference for a certain mode of conduct (such as honesty or aggressiveness), and a terminal value refers to preferences concerning desirable end-states of existence (such as peace or salvation). Values, whether positive or negative, designating desirable and undesirable modes and ends of action, are persistent through time and possess an observable consistency. They may be explicit (stated overtly in a value judgment) or implicit (inferred from nonverbal behavior), and they may be individually held or seen as part of a cultural pattern or system.[23]

Values in a Hierarchy

In Chapter 1, we alluded to the individual's need to maintain a balanced physiological and psychological state, a condition of homeostasis. Any basic need not satisfied in the individual sets his body in motion in order to reattain balance. To understand why values are so integrally related to needs, we must first understand the manner in which needs form a "hierarchy of prepotency." According to Maslow,[24] we can place needs on a continuum from the most potent to the least potent. In this hierarchy of needs the lower ones dominate all else if they remain unsatisfied: level 6, desire to know and understand; level 5, self-actualization needs; level 4, esteem needs; level 3, love needs; level 2, safety needs; level 1, physiological needs.

William Catton explains the functioning of this prepotency hierarchy: "A person may be obsessed with food, but only a relatively well-fed person is likely to become obsessed with working out a theory of valuing."[25] When we are hungry, then, it is difficult to engage in activity leading to self-actualization or knowledge and understanding. These needs come into play in terms of motivating our behavior only when our most basic drives are satisfied.

Values are related to this need hierarchy; they constitute the individual's or culture's concept of the best way to satisfy such needs. For example, if I am hungry, there are several ways in which I can satisfy my need to eat. I can buy, beg, borrow, or steal my food. The course of action that I choose will be dictated by the value I hold regarding the desirable means of satisfying my need. My value hierarchy, however, will dictate that I try all other means possible before I turn to the last resort of stealing. On the other hand, if I am a member of the counterculture of thieves, my value system probably will be such that I shall choose to steal my food first.

The value systems of individuals and cultures thus differ in terms of priorities and the value hierarchy employed by individuals to dictate appropriate action. Each individual has a particular value hierarchy that may differ from that of others. The terminal value of peace, for example, is ostensibly held by almost everyone; that is, most people tend to give lip service to the desirability of maintaining peace as a desirable end-state of existence. For some war-weary individuals, peace is the most important terminal value and must be achieved at all costs. For others, the price of peace may be too high, and other values such as nationalism, patriotism, and honor assume a higher place on the value hierarchy than does the end-state of peace.

Values thus constitute the concepts held by individuals and groups concerning the most desirable means of fulfilling one's needs. As such, values are one of the most crucial variables in the determination of human action and interaction.

Group Values

In Chapter 4 dealing with roles, we discussed how cultures are defined and preserved by their norms and standards of behavior, or, in terms of this chapter, by the set of values their members share regarding the desirable means and ends of action. Values determine trends toward consistency in behavior whether on an individual or group level. According to Kluckhohn, "a personal value is the private form of a group or universal value. It is not entirely unique to one personality, but it has its own special shadings, emphases and interpretations."[26] A group value, on the other hand, is held by "some plurality of individuals, whether this be a family, clique, association, tribe, nation or civilization. Group values consist in socially sanctioned ends and socially approved modes and means."[27] Whereas each group of people has a set of values distinct to that group, no two individuals in that group share identical values. The more homogeneous the culture, subculture, or counterculture, the more personal and group values tend to converge.

In a culturally heterogeneous society, on the other hand, values tend to conflict from individual to individual and group to group. Aberle[28] suggests that, in order to live in a culturally heterogeneous environment, certain crucial values must be shared by all members. For example, in a society of extreme religious diversity, religious tolerance must be a central value; otherwise those in power would end the diversity. In a mobile society such as ours, in which individuals move freely and frequently from one part of the country to another, a common concept of how to treat and react to strangers is necessary in order to preserve the ability to remain mobile.

Likewise, in the interracial situation certain values must be shared by participants in order that communication may proceed. For example, communicators must share the value that it is desirable for members of various races to come together on an intellectual if not a social level. There must be consensus among communicators that it is desirable to hear what others of different backgrounds and philosophies have to say. The interracial group members must share the notion that it is desirable to face and solve the interracial problems confronting participants. Although it is not necessary for all group members to desire complete integration of the races, if the communicators all believed in total segregation, we would have no interracial communication, at least on a face-to-face level. The bare value sharing necessary for interracial communication to begin and continue is a common understanding of the desirability of coming together, or listening to what others unlike ourselves have to say, and of solving the interracial problems of the society. For those who refuse to acknowledge the existence of a problem, the necessity for interracial interaction, or the desirability of hearing diverse opinions, there can be no productive interracial communication.

Value Conflict and Interracial Communication

Conflict in value systems is another major cause of communication breakdown in interracial settings. Theodore Balgooyen presents an excellent example of this type of conflict in his analysis of the clash in values existing between the American Plains Indians and the U.S. Commissioners of Indian Affairs who attempted to effect peace treaties with the various tribes. In his analysis Balgooyen demonstrates how such a conflict in values can make productive communication impossible:

Indians	Commissioners
1. Men should make peace to exchange gifts and trade.	1. Nations should make peace to establish property boundaries.
2. Men should dedicate life to gaining war honors.	2. Men should dedicate life to making the world secure.
3. Every man has the right to decide whom he shall obey.	3. Majority rules.
4. Only Indians belong living on the plains.	4. Indians ought to be moved to remote areas within defined boundaries.
5. Plains should not be settled but left in a natural state.	5. Plains should be settled and made productive.
6. The white race is inferior to the red race.	6. The red race is inferior to the white race.[29]

From this analysis it becomes apparent why the treaties effected between these two groups have been constantly broken. All the communication between these two cultures was based on conflicting value premises, both instrumental and terminal. The same conflict persists today; in New Mexico Indians are attempting to preserve the natural beauty of their land by opposing the smoke-belching power plants and strip mining designed to furnish the enormous urban centers of the West with power. The value conflict is basic: electric lights versus clean air and an undisturbed countryside; "progress" versus "conservation."

The previous study assumes that there existed an "Indian value system" and a "white man's value system" and that these two systems came into conflict when representatives of the two cultures met to effect agreement. The question remains of whether or not there exists in the United States a relatively unchanging set of values shared by most contemporary Americans. Steele and Redding assert that such a value system does exist and that it is possible to formulate these values into clusters of assertions.[30] They present the following nouns as examples of the values held by most Americans: puritan-pioneer morality, individualism, achievement of success, change and progress, ethical equality, equality of opportunity, optimism, efficiency and pragmatism, rejection of authority, scientific and secular rationality, sociality, material comfort, quantification, external conformity, humor, generosity, and patriotism.

Given the extensive heterogeneous qualities of American society, the Steele-Redding value analysis appears to be a vast oversimplification. The United States is composed of a large number of groups—including subcultures and countercultures. One outstanding example that constitutes an exception to this generalization of values is the "youth culture." In the rhetoric of the youth movement, members of the counterculture have seriously questioned the traditional values of American society as outlined by Steele and Redding. Although they tend to endorse the democratic principles advocated by their elders, they opine that these principles have never been put into practice for the entire population. They tend to reject material and worldly values in favor of a return to nature, condemning wealth and status as irrelevant to modern man. Whereas certain of their drug-oriented and sexual behaviors would suggest that members of the youth counterculture have rejected ascetic values regarding prudence and abstinence, the simplicity of existence advocated by many group members indicates the acceptance of a certain type of asceticism. Rather than "beating the drum" for individualism, as is common in the more establishment-oriented members of the society, these young people tend to reject principles of individualism in favor of an emphasis on communal living and group cooperation. They have also rejected the rationalistic and empirical emphases the sciences have introduced in favor of inquiry into the mystical and spiritual as exemplified by the increasing popularity of scientology and astrology. Finally the utilitarian and pragmatic values so commonly associated with the American culture have been replaced by a firm idealism in the hierarchy of values of the culture of the young.

Franklin Murphy, former Chancellor of UCLA, explained this value conflict between generations in his 1968 commencement address. In the eighteenth century, according to Murphy, the all-encompassing value was *"cogito ergo sum"* ["I think; therefore I am"], with an emphasis on rational thought. The elders of this present generation have embraced the value of *"fatio ergo sum"* ["I do; therefore I am"], with the value of achievement and productivity the all-pervasive guide to human behavior. Finally today's youth have turned to the notion of *"sentio ergo sum"* ["I feel; therefore I am"], with love, compassion, and brotherhood becoming the touchstones of the culture. Today's youth, according to Murphy, are concerned not with the bedroom and bathroom morality that so occupied their parents but with humanity. "We had to destroy the village to save it" is to them the contemporary obscenity. Thus the American value system as "a body of relatively unchanging values shared by most of the contemporary Americans" does not really exist. What does exist is a series of values and systems of values held by individuals and by groups in a complex society. Value systems within our society differ widely from race to race, from culture to culture, and from generation to generation.

Nancy Young in a study conducted to determine the development of values and value assimilation regarding the Chinese in Hawaii found, through a value analysis of young and old Chinese in Hawaii, that the complete assimilation of Chinese in Hawaii predicted by the psychologists in the past decades is not occurring. (Assimilation was here defined as the "unilateral approximation of one culture in the direction of the other.") Values related to success, hypothetical expenditures, family systems, and interethnic relations were investigated, and it was demonstrated that although the young Chinese had substantially different values from their elders, they also had a value system that was significantly different from that of the white population of the same age and geographical area.[31]

Value conflicts are thus indigenous to communication in heterogeneous groups and, most particularly, in interracial groups. Such conflict is particularly intrusive in communication between members of a culture and a counterculture. In such cases, obvious differences exist in the terminal values held by each: peace versus American dominance, freedom versus order, property rights versus individual rights, capitalism versus communism, and the individual versus the group. Conflicts also become apparent in instrumental values: violence versus nonviolence, "do your own thing" versus conformity, inner-directed action versus outer-directed action, self versus other, equality versus privilege, integration versus segregation, personal responsibility versus social welfare, liberalism versus conservatism, and right versus left. The issues on which individuals from diverse backgrounds can differ are almost endless. Nevertheless, it must be remembered that although such differences will always exist in a heterogeneous society, without some degree of value sharing no interracial communication is possible. Unless we can agree to disagree, interracial interaction becomes fruitless and futile.

EFFECTS OF BELIEFS, ATTITUDES, AND VALUES ON BEHAVIOR

Socialization

Throughout this chapter we have emphasized the importance of beliefs, attitudes, and values in interracial communication settings by alluding to the impact these communicator attributes have on the behavior of the communicator in interracial interaction. Society teaches us beliefs, attitudes, values, which in turn dictate our behavior. This process of "socialization" (as defined in Chapter 4) eventually controls individual behavior. As Arthur Cohen suggests regarding the impact of beliefs, attitudes, and values on human behavior:

Most of the investigators whose work we have examined make the broad psychological assumption that since attitudes are evaluated predispositions, they have consequences for the way people act toward others, for the programs they actually undertake, and for the manner in which they carry them out. Thus, attitudes are always seen as precursors of behavior, as determinants of how a person will actually behave in his daily affairs.[32]

Sherif and Cantril also emphasize the impact of beliefs, attitudes, and values on human behavior: "The socialization which occurs when an individual becomes a member of a group consists mainly in the achievement of conformity in experience and behavior to social values, standards, or norms already established. And the process of achieving conformity is, if we analyze it closely, nothing more or less than the formulation of appropriate attitudes in relation to these socially standardized values or norms or other criteria of conduct."[33] Not only does attitude influence behavior; behavior can also affect an individual's attitude. Bem,[34] for example, suggests that people look at their behavior to determine their attitudes. Individuals rely on external cues to determine internal states: "Most people agree that the question 'Why do you eat brown bread?' can be properly answered with "Because I like it.' I should like to convince you, however, that the question 'Why do I like brown bread?' frequently ought to be answered with 'Because I eat it.' "[35] This theory is closely related to that of Leon Festinger's "cognitive dissonance."[36] In order to maintain a psychological state of balance, the individual must feel that his behavior is in line with his concept of what is good and appropriate behavior. Consequently, if he habitually eats brown bread, he no doubt will explain his persistent actions by developing a positive attraction (an attitude) toward brown bread. Kresler, Nesbett, and Zanna's experiment supports Bem's hypothesis that under certain experimental conditions individuals infer their own beliefs from their overt behavior ("I eat it, therefore, I must like it").[37]

Major problems arise in attempting to infer attitudes and beliefs from the behavior of others and in predicting what behavior will ensue as soon as an individual's beliefs are known. Sarnoff and Katz suggest that this difficulty in predicting behavior from attitudes is based on the fact that behavior results from numerous intrapersonal and interpersonal forces that may be totally exclusive of the relevant attitude. In order to predict accurately the behavioral outcome of any single attitude, it would theoretically be necessary to collect data regarding those forces causing an individual to act.[38] Rokeach states: "If one focuses only on an attitude toward an object, he is bound to observe some inconsistency between attitudes and behavior, or at least a lack of dependence of behavior on attitude."[39]

This observable inconsistency between expressed beliefs and overt behavior is one of the major obstacles affecting interracial communication. "It is a well known fact that a man's actual beliefs and attitudes about a particular topic are only one set of the potential determinants of his verbal behavior. People sometimes lie or reveal only part of what they believe to be true."[40] When the subjects in the restaurant study claimed in an impersonal situation that they did not serve nonwhites, and in an actual face-to-face situation did serve nonwhites, they exhibited this inconsistency between belief-attitude and behavior.

Such an inconsistency between belief and behavior is important in the interracial communication context, because the interracial history of the United States is one of a proliferation of inconsistent behavior, particularly on the part of whites towards nonwhites. This incongruity between the spoken public value and the actual public action taken toward nonwhites has bred hostility, profound disillusionment, and keen resentment in those most deeply affected by the inconsistency. What we term here incongruence between publicly stated beliefs and public action many nonwhites call hypocrisy. This lack of congruence has occurred on a national level as promises of better education, food, housing, job opportunities, and civil rights are compared with the frequent obstacles put forth against these measures by the leaders of the establishment institutions. This inconsistency has also occurred on an individual level, when men and women who claim to be liberal and unprejudiced vote to maintain segregated housing and schools.

A survey conducted by the author reveals some results that might prove shocking to most northern and western whites who have long prided themselves on their lack of racial bias and their superiority over the bigotry of the southern white. In Los Angeles, sixty-five blacks who had moved to the city from the South were questioned on whether they trusted a white southerner more than a white northerner. Eighty-two percent agreed that because white southerners openly expressed their racial attitudes and conformed to those attitudes in their behavior, they were more predictable than northern whites and hence could be trusted more to behave consistently. These subjects expressed a disillusionment with the North and a desire to return to the South.

Thus, whereas the attitude of "racism" is in itself a barrier to interracial communication, the hypocrisy surrounding its expression is even more disrupting. The black subjects sampled would rather interact with an obvious racist who behaves in accordance with his openly stated beliefs than they would with one who expresses one belief and behaves in a manner contrary to that expression. The lack of trust so prevalent in interracial interaction is in great measure based on the realization of the incongruity between expressed beliefs, attitudes, and values and actual behavior.

INTERPERSONAL ATTRACTION: RACE OR BELIEF?

General Balance Theory

If communicators are of different races, the question arises concerning which is more important in interpersonal attraction, congruity of race between the communicators or congruity of belief? Are we attracted to communicate with someone because: (1) they are of the same race as we are or (2) they believe as we do?

Before we can answer this important interracial communication question, we must first review certain principles of interpersonal attraction which apply to *all* communication situations. According to Theodore Newcomb, individuals in a communication situation desire to maintain a state of psychological balance. His primary assumption is that communication among individuals performs the essential function of "enabling two or more individuals to maintain a simultaneous orientation toward one another as communicators and toward objects of communication."[41] According to Newcomb individuals who communicate freely with one another tend to resemble each other in attitudes toward objects of interest to both. To maintain social balance there seems to be a push among communicators toward a symmetry of orientation in beliefs, attitudes and values. Such a relationship is expressed as follows with A and B the communicators and X the subject of the communication.

$$
\begin{array}{cc}
X & X \\
+ \quad + & - \quad - \\
A + B & A + B
\end{array}
$$

This represents a symmetrical relationship with both A and B liking each other and agreeing in their orientation toward X. If an unbalanced relationship should develop, for example:

$$
\begin{array}{c}
X \\
- \quad + \\
A + B
\end{array}
$$

a pressure develops among the communicators either to change their attitudes toward X and reestablish symmetry of orientation or to change attitudes toward each other:

$$
\begin{array}{c}
X \\
- \quad + \\
A - B
\end{array}
$$

The perception and actual achievement of such symmetry varies with the intensity of the attitude toward X and the attraction the communicators feel toward each other. According to Newcomb, then, we are attracted to those who share X with us; if an asymmetrical orientation toward X should develop and we are still attracted to our cocommunicator, we shall feel the need to change our orientation or the orientation of our receiver to reestablish balance. In short we communicate to those with whom we feel an attraction about something that attracts us.

Symmetry in the Interracial Setting

Now that we have reviewed the basic principles on which interpersonal attraction and communication is based, we can attempt to answer the previous question: Which attraction is stronger, race congruity or belief congruity? Rokeach[42] conducted an experiment to answer this question of interpersonal attraction; he found that subjects in various environments chose partners on the basis of congruity of belief rather than on congruity of race. According to Rokeach, racial discrimination as a force in interpersonal choice has been greatly overemphasized: Belief discrimination is the more potent element in interpersonal attraction. He specified one key exception to his finding: Belief is the stronger attractive force only when pressure to discriminate racially is not strong or institutionally sanctioned. In such cases belief congruency becomes irrelevant.

Triandis and Davis[43] in another study testing the same question of attractive forces attack Rokeach's assertion that belief congruence is the most potent attractive mechanism. They assert that belief congruence is an important attractive force in interracial settings only in the case of close social distance friendships. Rokeach's findings are not indicative of the wide range of racial prejudice at work. Where there is a wide social distance, say Triandis and Davis, racial congruence is the stronger force in interpersonal attraction.

Rokeach responded to the Triandis-Davis assertion by stating that the treatments in the two experiments were not comparable, and hence the results could not be compared. He further asserted that, "All our data and Triandis' are consistent with the following proposition: the more salient a belief, the more will belief congruence override racial or ethnic congruence as a determinant of social distance."[44] Rokeach and Rothman sum up the concept of belief congruence as follows:

The principle of belief congruence asserts that we tend to value a given belief subsystem or system of beliefs in proportion to their degree of congruence with our own belief system and further, that we tend to value people in proportion to the degree to which they exhibit belief subsystems or systems of beliefs congruent with our own.[45]

In an attempt to determine the impact of degrees of racial prejudice on the question of the relative attractive forces of racial versus belief congruity, Byrne and Wong[46] conducted an experiment in which they found that high-prejudiced subjects assumed a greater attitude dissimilarity between themselves and black strangers than between themselves and white strangers. Low-prejudiced persons showed no differences between assumed attitude dissimilarity on a racial basis. Regardless of race or degrees of prejudice, in all subjects similarity of attitudes resulted in a positive rating for the stranger and dissimilarity of attitudes in a negative rating. This supplies further evidence that we are attracted to those who believe as we do. As Jones suggests: "Belief is the most important general criterion for interpersonal attraction (within a limited range of social distance). However, a willingness to make inferences about belief dissimilarity solely on the basis of race seems to characterize the prejudiced person."[47] Another study by Smith, Williams, and Willis supported the Byrne-Wong findings when it discovered that with the southernmost white subjects, race was the most important factor in interpersonal choice. In all other cases belief congruity was the most important factor.[48]

Finally a study conducted by Stein, Hardyck, and Smith[49] set out to examine Rokeach's contention that prejudice is a result of perceived dissimilarity of belief systems. Their results showed that, when information of beliefs was provided, subjects made choices on the basis of belief congruence. When no information on beliefs was provided, subjects made interpersonal choices on the basis of race. Subjects chose those of their same race, assuming that they would hold congruent beliefs and that members of another race would hold dissimilar beliefs. The less the white subjects knew of the belief systems of blacks, the more negative were their judgments regarding blacks.

The results of all these studies can be summarized as follows:

1. Belief congruence is the most frequent determinant of interpersonal attraction (we like those who like what we life).
2. If we know only that a person is of a different race, we assume he has different beliefs and judge him negatively.
3. Prejudiced persons tend to assume belief dissimilarity of blacks more frequently than do persons judged to be nonprejudiced.[50]

Jones suggests the implications of these findings for interracial communication:

The implications of these studies are clear for our analysis of social contact as a means of reducing intergroup hostilies. If through contact one removes the need to guess about the beliefs of blacks (and vice versa), presumably erroneous negative judgment will be diminished. Through interracial contact, greater belief similarity would be revealed, and racial hostilities based on assumed belief dissimilarity would be diminished.[51]

This discussion has demonstrated the importance of belief congruity in all interpersonal attraction and communication, including interracial interaction. According to Newcomb we all tend, when attracted to a person in a communication situation, to adjust our beliefs to achieve symmetry. Given this occurrence, Jones assumes that increased contact between the races will diminish faulty assumptions about belief dissimilarity between the races. This is quite true, but the question Jones tends to ignore is that dealing with a genuine, not a misinterpreted, dissimilarity of beliefs, attitudes, and values, which frequently manifests itself in the interracial communication setting and which threatens to pull the communicators, *A* and *B*, apart to the point where no further communication can take place.

X (busing)

− +

A (white)   +   B (black)

This lack of belief congruence, if held firmly and if of importance to both *A* and *B*, can result in the following:

X (busing)

− +

A − B

In this case, the beliefs were held so strongly that the initial attraction between *A* and *B* was destroyed by the asymmetry of their respective orientations to *X*, the busing question. Despite Jones's praise of interracial contact as a means of clearing up misconceptions, it should also be remembered that interracial communication can and frequently does reveal true divergence of opinion. Given the common desire to be with those who believe as we do, the divergence in individual and cultural beliefs, attitudes, and values often uncovered in the interracial setting also constitutes one of the major causes of interracial communication tension, hostility, and ultimate breakdown. Thus although interracial communication can bring participants closer together through the removal of misconceptions based on interpersonal ignorance, the interracial setting also provides the communicators with the opportunity to lock horns in value combat.

DISRUPTIVE BELIEFS, ATTITUDES, AND VALUES IN INTERRACIAL COMMUNICATION

In all intercultural communication, we assume there to be normal cutural variations in beliefs, attitudes, and values that tend to separate people of heterogeneous backgrounds. When a North American anthropologist engages in a discussion with a South American Indian, he discovers that the Indian holds beliefs that are unique to him and at variance with those held by the majority of North Americans. This belief disparity in the intercultural communication situation (characterized by the *lack* of a previous colonial relationship between the communicators) does not necessarily disrupt the interaction. On the contrary, the discovery of just such unique beliefs, attitudes, and values is frequently the aim of those participating in intercultural communication, a process that can best be described as consisting of a spirit of inquiry rather than advocacy.

Interracial and countercultural communication (communication in which the participants have coexisted in some type of colonial or paternalistic relationship), on the other hand, is characterized more often by a special and extreme divergence in beliefs, attitudes, and values, which at times makes it impossible for the communicators to overcome normal differences existing between peoples of diverse origins.

Attitude, Value, and Belief Divergence Among Races

Despite the Jones hypothesis that interracial communication can be helpful in eliminating erroneous assumptions of belief dissimilarity between the races, the fact remains that some disparity does exist in beliefs, attitudes, and values between communicators of different racial backgrounds. Survey studies reveal, given certain samples, that real and significant differences exist in the beliefs and attitudes held by blacks and whites with regard to certain contemporary issues. Campbell and Shuman,[52] in a survey study conducted throughout fifteen American cities with 2,814 black subjects and 2,945 white subjects, found a significant difference in the attitudes of the two races regarding riots. Whites believed that riots are planned by the ghetto community for the purposes of looting, that such action is harmful to the black cause, and that such civil disruptions could and should be prevented through the imposition of police control. Blacks in the study depicted riots as spontaneous outbreaks, as more helpful than harmful to the black cause, and as capable of being prevented through better employment opportunities. Many more blacks than whites in the sample blamed poor jobs and poor housing on racial discrimination.

In another survey study, W. Wilson compared black and white attitudes toward civil rights. He found significant differences in the specific values of the subjects, with the whites of the sample ranking law enforcement high and equal rights low in their value priorities, and the blacks ranking law enforcement low and equal rights high. In his summary he states: "This profound degree of both perceived and actual disagreement does not harken well for the future course of race relations."[53]

Rodolfo Medina,[54] a consultant on Anglo–chicano relations for the Department of Health, Education and Welfare in Los Angeles, presents an analysis of the value conflict he feels is responsible for chicano failure in the educational institutions of the dominant society. According to Medina, the chicano is less concerned with upward mobility than the Anglo; he is basically noncompetitive, is close to his family, and remains removed from the outside community. He also possesses strong male-female distinctions not common to the rest of the community. In his analysis Medina suggests that the value system of the chicano dooms him to failure in white schools where he must compete with the institutionally reinforced value systems of the white students.

Not all research in this area reveals agreement on the degree of this value disparity between the races. Rokeach and Parker[55] studied the value systems of a nationally drawn black and white sample that constituted a cross section of various socioeconomic statuses of the society. They found substantial similarities among black and white values. This author conducted a limited survey at the University of California, where seventy-five blacks and seventy-five whites were given an attitude inventory covering positions on various social, moral, religious, economic, and political issues. One-half of each sample was under 30 and one-half over 30. The results of this study revealed a greater similarity between blacks under 30 and whites under 30 than between whites under 30 and whites over 30. This generational gap did not exist in the all-black sample. The findings seem to suggest that a behavior study might reveal a greater generational value gap than a racial value disparity.

Problematic Attitudes and Value Structures in Interracial Communication

The attitudes tested in these studies were concerned with specific orientations toward specific issues. Underlying a viewpoint on any given issue, however, is a generalized value structure that permeates all interracial issues and constitutes one of the foundations of interracial conflict. In order to understand which generalized attitudes are most likely to ignite the flames of interracial hostility, it is helpful to delineate them and analyze how and why they are so disruptive to interracial communication.

The first set of attitudes are those held by the inhabitants of A in the scheme of interracial interaction. Those who inhabit the A space of a given society, it will be remembered, are those in power, those who control the major institutions of the society. In the United States, A is occupied by white inhabitants. One of the most destructive attitudes held and expressed by A members in the interracial setting is that of *racism*. Racism is a complex intertwining of beliefs of racial superiority, negative racial attitudes, and a value structure that supports actions maintaining racial superiority. Racism is expressed on three levels: *individual racism, institutional racism,* and *cultural racism.*

"Individual racism is closest to race prejudice and suggests a belief in the superiority of one's own race over another and the behavioral enactments that maintain those superior and inferior positions."[56] Black power spokesman Stokely Carmichael defined individual racism as "overt acts by individuals causing death, injury, or violent destruction of property."[57] These acts as described by Carmichael are preceded by and based on racist attitudes, which, when expressed, even in the most subtle or unconscious fashion in the interracial setting, disrupt the productivity of the process.

Institutional racism is seen by Jones as an extension of individual racist thought. It is "the conscious manipulation of institutions to achieve racist ends."[58] An example of such manipulation that restricts "on a racial basis the choices, rights, mobility and access of groups of individuals"[59] is college entrance-test scores.

Such scores tend to favor those students from white middle-class backgrounds and educations while diminishing the chances of nonwhite lower-economic-class students to enter institutions of higher education. In an interracial setting, communication that promotes or condones institutional racism produces bristle responses highly destructive to the outcome of the interaction.

The third type of racism disruptive to the interracial communication process is cultural racism. This belief and attitude assumes superiority of both culture and race. It constitutes "the individual and the institutional expression of the superiority of one race's cultural heritage over that of another race."[60] Cultural racism exists when cultural differences demonstrated by certain members of the society are negatively reinforced by those in power and when the cultural contributions of an entire group or race are overlooked in the educational system of the society. As Jones states:

It is not just black people who have been victimized by the cultural melting pot myth, but all ethnic minorities. White western European religion, music, philosophy, law, politics, economics, morality, science, and medicine are all without question considered to be the best in the world.[61]

Robert Allen presents a brief history of the behavioral expression of cultural racism (also known as cultural imperialism) in the United States. It is not difficult to understand why contemporary expressions of such racist attitudes in an interracial setting prove to be abrasive to those who feel they have long been the victims of cultural rape:

Family life and community are disrupted and traditional cultural forms fall into disuse. Under domestic colonialism, this process is even more destructive. Slave families were completely shattered and cultural continuity almost completely disrupted. The blacks who were kidnapped and dragooned to these shores were not only stripped of most of their cultural heritage, they soon lost the knowledge of their native African languages. They were forced to speak in the tongue of the masters and to adapt to the master's culture. In short, blacks were the victims of a pervasive cultural imperialism which destroyed all but faint remnants of the old African forms.[62]

Another attitude closely related to that of cultural racism or cultural imperialism which finds expression in interracial settings is that based on *colonialism.* The *American College Dictionary* defines colonialism in the traditional sense as "the policy of a nation seeking to extend or retain its authority over other nations or people."[63] If one views the United States as two nations, as James Baldwin does in *Another Country,* with one nation occupied by whites and the other by nonwhites, one can see how the nonwhite population could see itself in a colonial relationship with the power structure of the white community. A colonial attitude implies feelings of power, superiority, and control. In interracial settings, this attitude is frequently expressed by nonwhites who feel that certain whites possess "social worker mentalities." Those whites who express the desire to "take up the white man's burden" and to go into the ghetto "to raise *them* to *our* level" most often meet impatience and hostility from the nonwhites whom they are trying to "help." Many nonwhite militants see the basic relationship existing between the whites and nonwhites of the United States as fundamentally colonial:

Urging that U.S. blacks internationalize their fight for freedom, Malcolm [X] contended that black people as victims of domestic colonialism should view their struggle in terms of the world-wide anti-colonial revolt, and he took concrete steps to make this more than mere rhetoric.[64]

Stokely Carmichael also expresses a keen sensitivity to the pervasive colonial attitude of white Americans: "To put it another way, there is no 'American dilemma,' because black people in this country form a colony, and it is not in the interests of the colonial power to liberate them."[65] It is based on the belief that blacks are in fact a colony within the white man's United States that Black Panthers justify arming themselves. They view the white law enforcers as an occupying force that is violating foreign territory and likewise see themselves as protectors of the community, in much the same fashion as the early American colonists viewed the British or the Algerians more recently viewed the French. Nonwhites in interracial settings are thus extremely sensitive to the colonial attitudes expressed by white communicators, and the expression of such attitudes is a frequent cause of interracial communication disruption. What makes this particular attitude conflict difficult is the lack of white awareness with reference to their colonial impulses. The white lady or gentleman who expresses the desire to go into the inner city to help "those poor children from culturally disadvantaged homes" feels he or she is being altruistic and rarely recognizes the racist implications of such a colonial attitude.

Another common white attitude frequently expressed in interracial settings is that of *paternalism.* Similar to the attitude of colonialism, paternalism is "the principle or practice, on the part of a government or of anybody or person in authority, of managing or regulating the affairs of a country or community, or of individuals, in the manner of a father dealing with his children."[66] The southern white attitude toward blacks has been notoriously paternalistic for centuries. Samuel Lubell states:

For southern whites, [Booker T.] Washington was immensely useful in their need for a show of paternalism. Washington was one Negro the South could afford to be nice to, even as later southerners would boast how "I always help my nigger friends out of scrapes."[67]

Paternalism, however, is not solely characteristic of southern white racial attitudes, for many northern whites, unconsciously, even innocently, fall into the "I must help them because *they* cannot help themselves" syndrome. Expressions of attitudes such as these in interracial communication situations elicit the same responses as any unjustified exertion of parental authority: resentment and rebellion.

If one were to attempt to sum up all these destructive interracial attitudes under an umbrella, it would not be difficult to see that at the core of racism, colonialism, and paternalism is the strong and stubborn thread of *chauvinism,* the attitude that consistently asserts, "Mine is best, I am best." Ruth Benedict describes this all-encompassing preoccupation with self:

But our achievements, our institutions are unique, they are of a different order from those of lesser races and must be protected at all costs. So that today, whether it is a question of imperialism, or of race prejudice, we are still preoccupied with the uniqueness, not of human institutions of the world at large, which no one has ever cared about anyway, but of our own institutions, and our own achievements. . . .[68]

This chauvinistic attitude is at the heart of most human conflict and most assuredly dooms its possessor to great strife in settings where he finds himself involved with individuals much different from himself. Perhaps the most destructive aspect of chauvinism is that it leads to reaction; when one is constantly told he is inferior, he tends to develop attitudes of superiority in self-defense.

"Defensiveness" best describes the quality of the attitudes held by the inhabitants of the *C* portion of the interracial environment diagram. Those not in power tend to *react to* those in power. The result is the development of a reverse racism and a defensive chauvinism on the part of *C* members. "No, mine is better" becomes the standard response to white cultural racism. An attitude of exclusiveness results: "O.K., Whitey, you set me apart; now you can't have any part of me or mine." This is best exemplified by the hostility blacks feel and express toward whites who wear "natural" hair styles or who use black code expressions such as "right on." The feeling here is that whites are again attempting to violate ethnic identity and preempt the culture of the race. Rather than fighting against the destructive force of all forms of chauvinism, members of *C* tend to respond to these white attitudes by developing an equally potent chauvinism; the result is the growth of a mutual hatred in the interracial setting. All hostile, condescending, and defensive attitudes expressed in the interracial communication situation, whether they are possessed by members of *A* or *C*, cause the most disappointing and bitter collapse of interracial interaction. Paralyzed by a mutually expressed hostility, communicators are totally unable to engage in any form of productive communication.

There is no simple effective solution to the enormous problem of interracial belief, attitude, and value conflict. Those motivated in an interracial setting to engage in productive communication must fight the basic tendency of all humans to possess an egocentrism regarding personal beliefs, attitudes, and values. Such a struggle against self does not necessitate a rejection of one's own value system or one's own perception of reality. We must realize, however, that what we hold to be true and real for us does not necessarily constitute the reality of another, particularly if that other is from a background far removed from our own. Empathy is perhaps the key to overcoming the shackles of our own belief and value systems: We must try in interracial settings to step outside ourselves in order to gain an understanding of the reality of others. This momentary suspension of self is very difficult but crucially important. The statement that must guide us is not "You are wrong, I'm right," but rather "You're right in your reality, I'm right in mine; where can we meet, if at all?"

Activities

1. Select a controversial topic dealing with race relations. As small interracial groups discuss this topic in front of the class, have the observers analyze on paper the conflicts that arise. Is the disagreement based on incongruent beliefs? If so, what kinds of beliefs are in dispute? Basic? Peripheral? Inconsequential? How might the discussants resolve this belief conflict? What values come into dispute? Are they instrumental or terminal values? Do members of the same race in the group tend to hold the same beliefs, attitudes, and values? What opposing realities are presented?

2. Construct a value questionnaire with at least three value statements in each of the following categories: political, economic, moral, educational, and social. Select statements which the class feels ought to produce disagreement between races. Allow each class member to administer this questionnaire to several members of his own race, both older and younger. Compare the results in class. Do the races really differ regarding these values? Do various age groups differ within a racial group more than the racial groups differ from each other? What difficulties are involved in making these assessments?

3. In daily conversation, interracial or intraracial, listen carefully and determine how many disagreements have belief and values conflict as the core cause. Which beliefs and values do people tend to argue most about? Why?

NOTES

1. Martin Fishbein and Bertram Raven, "The AB Scales: An Operational Definition of Belief and Attitude," *Human Relations* 15 (1962): 42.
2. Daryl J. Bem, *Beliefs, Attitudes, and Human Affairs* (Belmont, Calif.: Brooks/Cole, 1970), p. 4.
3. Milton Rokeach, *Beliefs, Attitudes, and Values* (San Francisco: Jossey, Bass, 1968), p. 2.
4. Ibid., p. 3.
5. Digby Diehl, "An Interview with Fred L. Hartley," *West Magazine* of *Los Angeles Times* (February 20, 1972), p. 30.
6. Richard Wright, *Black Boy* (New York: Harper & Row, 1966), p. 21.
7. Bem, op. cit., p. 14.

8. Philip Zimbardo and Ebbe B. Ebbesen, *Influencing Attitudes and Changing Behavior* (Reading, Mass.: Addison-Wesley, 1970), p. 6.

9. Muzafer Sherif and Hadley Cantril, "The Psychology of Attitudes, Part I," *Psychol. Rev.* 52 (1945): 295–319.

10. T. M. Newcomb, "On the Definition of Attitude," in M. Jahoda and N. Warren, *Attitudes: Selected Readings* (Baltimore: Penguin, 1966), p. 22.

11. Rokeach, op. cit., pp. 112, 159.

12. Daniel Katz, "The Functional Approach to the Study of Attitude," *Public Opinion Quarterly* 24 (1966), pp. 163–204.

13. Richard T. La Piere, "Attitudes vs. Actions," *Social Forces* 13 (1934): 230–237.

14. Sherif and Cantril, op. cit., p. 306.

15. Muzafer Sherif and Carl Hovland, *Social Judgement* (New Haven: Yale University Press, 1961), p. 5.

16. Rokeach, op. cit., p. 126.

17. La Piere, op. cit., pp. 230–237.

18. Bernard Kutner, Carol Wilkins, and Penny Yarrow, "Verbal Attitudes and Overt Behavior Involving Racial Prejudice," *J. Abnorm. Soc. Psychol.* 47 (1952): 629–652.

19. Rokeach, op. cit., p. 161.

20. Ibid.

21. Clyde Kluckhohn et al., "Values and Value Orientation in the Theory of Action," in Talcott Parsons and Edward Shils, *Toward a General Theory of Action* (Cambridge, Mass.: Harvard University Press, 1954), p. 395.

22. Bem, op. cit., p. 16.

23. Ethel Albert, "The Classification of Values: A Method and Illustration," *Amer. Anthrop.* 58 (1956): 221–222.

24. A. H. Maslow, "A Theory of Human Motivation," *Psychol. Rev.* 50 (1943): 393.

25. William R. Catton, Jr., "A Theory of Value," *Amer. Soc. Rev.* 24 (1959): 310–317.

26. Kluckhohn et al., op. cit., p. 416.

27. Ibid., p. 17.

28. David Aberle, "Shared Values in Complex Societies," *Amer. Soc. Rev.* 15 (1950), 495–501.

29. Theodore Balgooyen, "A Study of Conflicting Values: American Plains Indian Orators vs. the U.S. Commissioners of Indian Affairs," *Western Speech* 26 (Spring 1962): 76–82.

30. Edward Steele and W. Charles Redding, "The American Value System: Premises for Persuasion," *Western Speech* 26 (Spring 1962): 83–91.

31. Nancy F. Young, "Values and Strategies Among Chinese in Hawaii," *Sociol. Soc. Res.* 56 (1972): 22–24.

32. Arthur R. Cohen, *Attitude Change and Social Influence* (New York: Basic Books, 1964), pp. 137–138.

33. Sherif and Cantril, op. cit.

34. Bem, op. cit., p. 54.

35. Ibid.

36. Leon Festinger, "Cognitive Dissonance," in Edward E. Sampson, *Approaches, Contents, and Problems of Social Psychology* (Englewood Cliffs, N.J.: Prentice-Hall, 1965), pp. 9–16.

37. Charles Kresler, Richard Nesbett, and Mark Zanna, "On Inferring One's Belief from One's Behavior," *J. Pers. Soc. Psychol.* 11 (1969): 321–327.

38. Irving Sarnoff and Daniel Katz, "The Motivational Basis of Attitude Change," *J. Abnorm. Soc. Psychol.* 49 (1962): 115–124.

39. Rokeach, op. cit., p. 531.

40. Dana Bramel, "Interpersonal Attraction, Hostility, and Perception," in *Experimental Social Psychology,* ed. Judson Mills (London: Macmillan, 1969), pp. 77–120.

41. Theodore Newcomb, "An Approach to the Study of Communicative Acts," *Psychol. Rev.* 60 (1953): 394.

42. Rokeach, op. cit., p. 62–81.

43. Harry C. Triandis and E. Davis, "Race and Beliefs and Determinants of Behavioral Intentions," *J. Pers. Soc. Psychol.* 2 (1965): 715–745.

44. Milton Rokeach, "Belief vs. Race as Determinants of Social Distance: Comment on Triandis Paper," *J. Abnorm. Soc. Psychol.* 62 (1961): 187.

45. Milton Rokeach and Gilbert Rothman, "The Principle of Belief Congruence and the Congruity Principle as Models of Cognitive Interaction," *Psychol. Rev.* 72 (1965): 128.

46. D. Byrne and Terry Wong, "Racial Prejudice, Interpersonal Attraction and Assumed Dissimilarity of Attitudes," *J. Abnorm. Soc. Psychol.* 65 (1962): 246–253.

47. James M. Jones, *Prejudice and Racism* (Reading, Mass.: Addison-Wesley, 1972), p. 84.

48. Carol R. Smith, L. Williams, and Richard Willis, "Race, Sex, and Belief as Determinants of Friendship and Acceptance," *J. Pers. Soc. Psychol.* 5 (1967): 127–137.

49. D. D. Stein, J. A. Hardyck, M. B. Smith, "Race and Belief: An Open and Shut Case," *J. Pers. Soc. Psychol.* 1 (1965): 281–289.
50. Jones, op. cit., p. 85.
51. Ibid., p. 84.
52. A. Campbell and H. Shuman, *Racial Attitudes in Fifteen American Cities* (Ann Arbor, Mich.: Institute for Social Research, 1969).
53. W. Wilson, "Rank Order of Discrimination and Its Relevance to Civil Rights Priorities," *J. Pers. Soc. Psychol.* 15 (1970): 121.
54. Rodolfo Medina, "The Chicano, Education, and Contrasting Values," *Los Angeles Times,* 6 April 1972, p. B 1.
55. M. Rokeach and S. Parker, "Values as Social Indicators of Poverty and Race Relations in America," *The Annals of the American Academy of Political and Social Science* 388 (1970): 97–111.
56. Jones, op. cit., p. 5.
57. Stokely Carmichael and Charles V. Hamilton, *Black Power* (New York: Random House, 1967), pp. 3–5.
58. Jones, op. cit.
59. Ibid., p. 6.
60. Ibid.
61. Ibid.
62. Robert L. Allen, *Black Awakening in Capitalistic America* (Garden City, N.Y.: Doubleday, 1969), p. 11.
63. *American College Dictionary* (New York: Random House, 1958), p. 239.
64. Allen, op. cit., p. 32.
65. Carmichael and Hamilton, op. cit., p. 5.
66. *American College Dictionary,* op. cit., p. 88.
67. Samuel Lubell, *White and Black* (New York: Harper & Row, 1964), p. 29.
68. Ruth Benedict, *Patterns of Culture* (Boston: Houghton Mifflin, 1934), p. 5.

6

Language and Interracial Communication

After a Harlem street rally, one of these downtown "leaders" and I were talking when we were approached by a Harlem hustler. To my knowledge I'd never seen this hustler before; he said to me, approximately: "Hey, baby! I dig you holding this all-originals scene at the track . . . I'm going to lay a vine under the Jew's balls for a dime—got to give you a play . . . Got the shorts out here trying to scuffle up on some bread . . . Well, my man, I'll get on, got to go peck a little, and cop me some z's—." And the hustler went on up Seventh Avenue.

I would never have given it another thought, except that this downtown "leader" was standing, staring after that hustler, looking as if he'd just heard Sanskrit. He asked me what had been said, and I told him. The hustler had said he was aware that the Muslims were holding an all-black bazaar at Rockland Palace, which is primarily a dancehall. The hustler intended to pawn a suit for ten dollars to attend and patronize the bazaar. He had very little money but he was trying hard to make some. He was going to eat, then he would get some sleep.[1]

Malcolm X's rendition of this interesting Harlem interaction exemplifies the importance of language in the interracial communication setting. We have thus far discussed several communication attributes that affect the outcome of interracial contacts; the communicator's stereotypes, perceptions, role expectations, beliefs, attitudes, and values all contribute to the success or failure of communication between members of different racial and ethnic groups. We now turn our attention to the actual means whereby all the above attributes are expressed. There are two basic means of communication: verbal and nonverbal symbols and actions. In this chapter we shall concentrate on the verbal means of interaction, namely, language, and the manner in which its uses and forms affect interracial communication. As Malcolm's description so well demonstrates, language—a miraculous possession of the human being—can serve both to unite and to separate people.

DEFINITION OF LANGUAGE

Language as Communication

Many linguists, sociolinguists, and psycholinguists see language essentially as a vehicle for interpersonal communication. Sapir regards language as "a purely human and non-instinctive method of communicating ideas, emotions, and desires by means of a system of voluntarily produced symbols."[2] He then sees language as a characteristically human attribute that is learned and voluntary. Language encompases a "system" or an organized structure of symbols. George Miller also sees language as a basic means of achieving interpersonal contact. "A language is a system of arbitrary vocal signs that can be used to obtain cooperation among the members of a social group."[3] He states further that "social process without communication is by definition impossible, and by all odds, the most important medium for communication is language."[4] Margaret Schaluch further emphasizes the communicative essence of language: "Language as communication implies community of living. A symbol is not a symbol; that is to say, it is not effective unless it is understood in approximately the same way by a group of people living and working together."[5]

Not all psycholinguists, however, endorse this notion that the essential function of language is to establish a means of interpersonal communication. DeVito disagrees with the definition of language as a system of symbols whose primary function is to communicate. "If there were but one person living, according to this definition, there could be no language because thought could not be communicated from one person to another."[6] He defines language as "a potentially self-reflexive, structured system of symbols which catalog the objects, events, and relations in the world."[7] Some theorists, then, see language as necessarily related to interpersonal communication; others, like DeVito, see it as a means by which the individual cognitively structures his world (this latter function appears to be essentially a means of intrapersonal communication). All seem to agree, however, that language consists of a series of conventionally agreed-on symbols and a means of organizing or arranging those symbols (a grammar). Symbols of something, of course, are "simply substitutions used to stand for that something."[8] Linguistic symbols may be expressed as articulated speech sounds or written forms.

Language, as a voluntarily produced and learned system of organizing socially agreed-on symbols of experience, serves many functions for human beings. As DeVito suggests, it functions as a means of aiding us in ordering our personal experiences within our consciousness, enabling us to communicate systematically with ourselves. Language also serves to facilitate community life and social processes by providing us with a mutually shared tool for interpersonal contact. By assigning conventional speech sounds or written symbols to human experience, we are able to express that experience to others. Finally language frees us from our environment, for, unlike lower species deprived of symbolic processes, humans need not be in the presence of an object in order to communicate something about that object. Through the use of language we carry that object and all its properties within our consciousness by means of the symbols we hold to stand for whatever we wish to think about and/or communicate.

The Effect of Language on Its Users
Language has a great effect on those who use it; the symbols we include and the system whereby we organize those symbols influence our thought patterns, perceptions, and behavior.

Language and thought   The degree to which language influences thought is a debatable question. Some suggest that "language and thought are completely separable and independent, that the language one speaks exerts no influence on thought whatever."[9] Others suggest that language and thought are essentially the same, that one cannot think without language and that the "language one speaks determines the thought one has."[10] Many support this latter position. Bruner believes that language is as essential to thought as it is to communication. He suggests that a person does not mature in intellectual capacity until he masters the symbolic use of language so he can "mentally manipulate his experience."[11] In his study of linguistic and thought processes, Bryson found that "symbolic systems do shape and determine our thought."[12] Stewart Chase maintains that ". . . language as it has developed is less influenced by reflection than thought is influenced by the accepted structure of language."[13] And Alexander maintains that the relationship between language and thought is reciprocal: ". . . language not only controls our thinking to some extent, but also our thinking does shape language."[14]

Perhaps the most famous statement regarding the relationship between thought and language is the Sapir-Whorfian hypothesis, which suggests that experience with our world is as it is, primarily because our language system predetermines that we make certain selections from the many possible interpretations of the environment.[15] According to Whorf concepts of time, space, and matter are not held in the same manner by all people; the differences are conditioned by the characteristics of the language we possess.[16]

Language and perception   If language structures and influences our thought patterns, it follows that by setting up certain environmental expectations language will also structure our perceptions of the world. Alexander suggests that "our linguistic symbol system can influence the way in which we see objects."[17] We tend to see those things for which we have symbols and perceive them in the manner dictated by the definitions offered by our language. DeVito describes this selective perception dictated by our language by comparing the objects and symbols of several cultures:

English, for example, has relatively few terms for horses—"horse," "pony," "mare," "stallion," and perhaps a few others. Arabic, on the other hand, has scores of terms, denoting the different kinds of breeds and conditions of horses, but no generic term corresponding to the English "horse." Similarly, Eskimo has no single term for snow but only numerous and distinct terms for different kinds of snow. Trobriand Islanders have dozens of terms for the different stages and qualities of yams. . . . An English speaker can see all the distinctions among horses that an Arabic speaker sees. It is simply that his language does not provide highly codable terms for these various nuances of differences. The important point is that the English speaker can make these distinctions (with adjectives, for example) but not as easily and quickly.[18]

According to Whorf, the Eskimo would be more sensitive to variations in snow and would actually perceive more differences, because his language allows him to conceive more easily of those differences. The Eskimo speaker and the English speaker are not inclined to see the same world, because their respective languages do not describe the world in the same fashion.

Language and behavior   Language not only influences the manner in which we think and the way in which we perceive our environment; it also influences our responses to our environment, that is, our actions. Differences in language have been demonstrated to cause differences in the ways in which people behave. DeVito cites various studies that compare behavioral differences between Hopi and English speakers based on linguistic differences.[19] Hopi and English speakers were asked to group two of three pictures together on similarity of subject matter; and they did so differently because their languages dictated a differential perception of similarity. The series of pictures showed: (1) a person frosting a cake, (2) a person painting a wall, (3) a person decorating a vase. The English speakers grouped the two pictures that showed the subjects painting (2 and 3) or the two pictures that presented the subjects engaged in decorating (1 and 3). The Indians grouped the two pictures in which the subjects appeared to be "smearing on a surface," for they have a special verb for that activity in their language (1 and 2).

Another such study was conducted on Navaho and English speakers. The English language emphasizes time and number, whereas the Navaho language emphasizes the characteristics of form. In another study children were asked to match two of three objects. The English-speaking children matched the objects according to color; the Navaho children, guided by their language, grouped the objects according to similarity in form.

We consciously perceive one attribute of our environment rather than another because we have a word to stand for it, and our system of symbols structures what we see and consequently how we behave. Cultures with different languages can thus be expected to perceive the world differently and exhibit different behavioral patterns.

Language as an Expression of Culture

Language serves both as an expression of culture and as an influence on the culture itself. "Language must be as old as the oldest of Man's cultural artifacts; it began when culture began and has developed continuously ever since."[20] Language can thus be viewed as an extension of culture. DeVito, for example, in his analysis of the linguistic differences between English, Arab, and Trobriand Island speakers, concludes that significant language differences are accurate gauges of significant cultural differences.

"Thus it seems reasonable to conclude that horses in Arabic culture, snow in Eskimo culture, and yams in the culture of the Trobriand Islanders are more important than they are in English speaking cultures."[21] Hoijer also suggests that language differences can be taken as a sign of cultural differences when he states that the Navahos' lack of a clear distinction between objects, subjects, and predicates in their language is reflected in their passive attitude toward life.[22] Linguistic studies conducted in England reveal that the different life opportunities of the various social classes in English society are reflected in the language used by those classes. Those of the lower working class have fewer life options; their language is restrictive in form and has few choices of expression available. The middle-class group members have more complex linguistic forms and a larger supply of symbolic and grammatical choices.[23]

As a cultural phenomenon language, of course, is learned. It is culturally induced and developed and as such reflects the values of the culture. Language enculturates an individual by predetermining how he sees the world. "The particular code a child learns exerts a powerful influence on his interaction with his environment. By specifying or highlighting what in the environment is relevant or irrevelent, the code influences the nature of the individual's experience."[24] This code is the possession of the group that employs it; ". . . it is an art that can be passed on from one generation to the next only by intensive education."[25] When the baby enters the world, he begins to perceive that those around him behave in rather stable ways toward objects in the environment, and he sees that adults in his world employ special linguistic patterns. Through the gradual development of his knowledge and use of language, the child eventually learns to behave in the manner set forth by his elders and hence comes to understand and participate in the culture.[26]

Language is not only an expression of culture and an influence on culture; it is also a means whereby culture proceeds and survives. Language acts as a unifying force within a culture by enabling individuals to make contact with others like themselves and to pass on cultural values. As Hoijer states: "Man's possession of language enables him to share the experiences and thoughts of his fellows and to re-create his personal experience for their benefit."[27] Bryson further emphasizes the function of language in perpetuating culture: ". . . symbol habits . . . are . . . the bonds that unite some persons in communal groups, shutting out others, controlling social relationships. . . ."[28] This social-cultural function of language as a means whereby we make contact with others is devastatingly portrayed in Dalton Trumbo's book and film *Johnny Got His Gun.* In these works Johnny, a soldier of World War I, is reduced to virtually a vegetable state as a result of wounds from an explosion and the ensuing surgery to save his life. His communication mechanisms, his ability to express any linguistic code to another human being in order to make any form of social contact are destroyed. He has lost his eyes, ears, nose, mouth, arms and legs and with them all means of perceiving his environment except his sense of physical feeling. Imprisoned within his own thoughts, he experiences an incomprehensible hell. Unable to verify his perceptions of reality through social contact with the outside world, he borders on insanity until he discovers he can communicate by pounding his head on his pillow in Morse code. Those observing him respond by tapping in Morse code on his forehead, and for better or worse, he is again in contact with his culture. Before his communication breakthrough, Johnny's inability to express a comprehensible code to the outside world reduced him to the stature of a nonhuman in the eyes of most of those caring for him, so essential is language in the maintenance of human cultural contact.

Language, then, our conventionally agreed-on system of symbols, codes our experience; enables us to communicate that experience to others; structures our thoughts, perceptions, and actions; and serves both as an expression of and an influence on our culture.

THE LANGUAGE OF RACISM

We have seen that language not only expresses ideas but also shapes attitudes; our linguistic habits predispose us to perceive reality based on the symbols we hold to stand for that reality. Racist language not only expresses racist attitudes; it helps to develop such attitudes in those learning the symbolic system. We shall now concentrate on the language of racism employed by white members of society, because: (1) coming from those in power, such language has a more profound effect on the society than does racist language employed by nonwhites; and (2) the language of white racism is essentially offensive in nature, whereas the racist language of nonwhites in our society is derived mainly from a defensive reaction. Nonwhite racist language will be discussed in the next section.

Language can have an enormous influence on the attitudes of those employing it. The process whereby language systems affect human cognitions may be completely unconscious and hence its influence may be totally overlooked by the users of the language. "Language can thus become an instrument of both propaganda and indoctrination for a given idea."[29] That racist language can affect the development of young minds has long been a postulate of anti-defamation groups. Coner describes the process:

The white Mississippi youngster who heard the late Senator Theodore Bilbo declare in a public speech that he did not want an egg from a black chicken or milk from a black cow, emphasizing his antagonism toward blacks, received preparation for the establishment of an extreme racist attitude. The suburban youngster in the city who pointed to a black youngster and said, "Look, Mommy, there is a baby maid," had received preparation through isolation for benign but nonetheless racist attitudes.[30]

The Nazis well understood the power of language in shaping racial attitudes. In order to justify the mass incarceration and eventual extermination of Jews to the German public, those in power had to effect a redefinition of Jews in the minds of the populace; it was through the manipulation of the language referring to Jews that such a change was effected. By constantly using violent and threatening adjectives to apply to the Jews over a long period of time, the Nazis were able to substitute the words for the objects in the minds of the German audiences. As Bosmajian points out: ". . . The Bolsheviks were not *like* dragons, they *were* a dragon; the Jews were not *like* a demon or bacillus, they *were* both demon and bacillus."[31]

Racist Language and the Power to Control

The example of Nazi word manipulation demonstrates the power inherent in the definition process. The power to define is the power to control, and those holding the reins of authority in any society can define the environment in order to remain in authority. Lerone Bennett, Jr., in quoting from *Alice in Wonderland,* demonstrates the power of word control:

"When I see a word," Humpty Dumpty said in a rather scornful tone, "It means just what I choose it to mean—neither more nor less."

"The question is," said Alice, "whether you can make words mean so many different things."

"The question is," said Humpty Dumpty, "which is the master—that is all."[32]

The question is: Who in our society is the master? That is, who has the power to control definitions and is responsible for the language of racism? There is no question that, at least at present, the white power structure dominates the most widely accepted linguistic definitions in our country. Although times are changing and the media are becoming more sensitive to the desire of various groups to define themselves, white standards of racism are nonetheless still in control of our language as it is used by the majority of the white population. This white standard is well expressed in an old folk song lyric that demonstrates the standards of desirability as defined by whites in the society:

"White, you're right
Light, you can fight
Brown, stand around
Black, stand back, stand back"[33]

Bosmajian places the blame for the language of white racism strongly within the white segment of society. He suggests that the use of derogatory terms such as "nigger" to refer to nonwhites gives whites power over the victims of such language usage. Most whites are hesitant to relinquish this power and view language as a personal extension; thus they regard attacks on their language as personal attacks. Bosmajian urges whites to eradicate racism by concentrating on the attitudes in their own communities, not by defining the problem as existing in the nonwhite areas of the nation. He urges whites to "clean up their language to rid it of words and phrases which connote racism to the blacks. . . ."[34] Being in power for so long, "whites of this nation have demonstrated little sensitivity to the language of racial strife. Whitey has for too long been speaking and writing in terminology, which, often being offensive to the blacks, creates hostility and suspicion and breaks down communication."[35] So strong is the power of definition that even the victims of racist language come to accept some of the terminology that aids in their own stereotyping. As Podair states: "Thus, even Negroes may develop speech patterns filled with expressions adding to the strengthening of stereotypes."[36]

The victims of racist language also realize the power of language and definition. Stokely Carmichael states: "I believe that people who can define are masters . . . the first need of a free people is to be able to define their own terms and have those terms recognized by their oppressors."[37] This increasing sensitivity on the part of the victims of racist language to the power of linguistic definition is keenly demonstrated by the desire of various nonwhite groups to change the names that are used to denote members of their groups and to establish their own linguistic definition of self rather than accept the definitions imposed upon them by the white power structure. United States residents of Mexican origin are demanding that they be called "chicano" rather than "Mexican," and residents whose predecessors were from Africa are shunning the terms "Negro" and "colored" as white-imposed designations and demanding that these words be replaced by the terms "black" and "Afro-American." Bennett presents an analysis of the complicated factors involved in the thrust toward a black redefinition:

. . . the pro-black contingent contends with Humpty Dumpty that names are the essense of the game of power and control. And they maintain that a change in name will short-circuit the stereotyped thinking patterns that undergird the system of racism in America. . . . A third group, composed primarily of Black Power advocates, has adopted a new vocabulary in which the word "black" is reserved for "black brothers and sisters who are emancipating themselves," and the word "negro" is used contemptuously for Negroes "who are still in whitey's bag and who stil think of themselves and speak of themselves as Negroes."[38]

Malcolm X was one of the first to popularize the need for a change in name for the American "Negro." He states:

During slavery days black men were given the names of their masters, like the branding of cattle. Smith, Jones, and Williams are not African names, they're Anglo-Saxon names that were forced upon the so-called Negro. Rather than bear the brand of a slave-master, we Muslims change our second names to X which is the Arabic symbol for the unknown. It removes the white man's stigma. . . . Not content with stripping us of our names, the white man, in his evilness, stripped us of our humanity . . . So the white man made up a special name for his slave animal— "Negro." It's a synthetic name that means low, filthy beast. We want no part of it.[39]

The victims of the language of racism in our society are thus well aware of the power of definition, and they are attempting to wrest that power from the white structure by reversing the trend of outwardly imposed designations and engaging in the process of self-definition. This process comprises one of the areas of conflict that frequently erupts in interracial communication settings. Bosmajian suggests that whites are, consciously or unconsciously, highly defensive of their language habits and are reluctant to relinquish the power that derives from controlling language. Whites frequently persist in interracial settings in employing terms that nonwhites regard as racist, often insisting on using the terms "colored" or "Negro" rather than adopting the designation "black" or "Afro-American." This insistence causes the kind of bristle responses, described in Chapter 2, that inevitably result in tension, hostility, and ultimate breakdown.

Examples of Racist Language

An outstanding example of the racist attitudes inherent in much language usage is revealed in the connotations associated with the words "black" and "white" in the English language. The notions of "black" as evil and "white" as good and pure are deeply embedded within the symbolism of the art and literature of our culture. Isaacs points out that these negative associations can be found in the Bible, in Milton, and in Shakespeare: ". . . They can be traced down the columns of any dichotomy from white hope to white wash, from the black arts to the Black Mass . . . 'I am black *but* comely,' sang the Shulamite maiden to the daughters of Jerusalem, and on that 'but' hangs a whole great skein of our culture."[40] William Blake's *The Little Black Boy,* a 1798 classic of English literature, is heavily laden with the racist overtones associated with the poet's references to "black" and "white."

My mother bore me in the Southern wild,
And I am black, but O! my soul is white;
White as an Angel is the English child,
But I am black, as if bereaved of light.

And the pathetic black child of the poem conceives of grace as turning from black to white, and being white as a prerequisite to being loved:

And then I'll stand and stroke his silver hair,
And be like him, and he will then love me.[41]

Bosmajian presents Martin Luther King's analysis of the black–white connotations of our language:

In Roget's *Thesaurus,* there are some 120 synonyms for blackness, and at least 60 percent of them are offensive—such words as "blot," "soot," "grime," "devil," and "foul." There are some 134 synonyms for "whiteness," and all are favorable, expressed in such words as "purity," "cleanliness," "chastity," and "innocence." A white lie is better than a black lie. The most degenerate member of the family is the "black sheep," not the "white sheep."[42]

Podair discusses the same topic and presents his analysis of the various connotations that white and black suggest in language:

Thus, "black looks" are defined as "sullen," "hostile," "foreboding"; "black cruelty" as "foully or outrageously wicked"; . . . In both dictionary and colloquial meanings, "black" has become linked up with all that mankind should eschew, while "white"—in most instances—has become the symbol of purity and goodness that we should embrace both as individuals and as a community.[43]

Such analyses, of course, always invite discussions of the exceptions in the language and it is important to remember that such exceptions do exist. Exceptions must be expected when one offers a gross generalization regarding meaning in language. Bosmajian presents examples of negative connotations of the term "white":

. . . "white" has numerous negative connotations: white livered (cowardly), white flag (surrender), white elephant (useless), white plague (tuberculosis), white wash (conceal), white feather (cowardice), etc. The ugliness and terror associated with the color white are portrayed by Melville in the chapter "The Whiteness of the Whale" in *Moby Dick.* At the beginning of the chapter, Melville says, "It was the whiteness of the whale that above all things appalled me."[44]

Despite these notable exceptions, there is systematic evidence to indicate that the term "black" projects a generally negative connotation and the term "white" a generally positive connotation among the users of the language. Mary Ellen Goodman conducted a semantic study among 103 children and found that the subjects associated dark skin color with darkness, death, and evil, but "white" was associated with clean, pleasant, pretty, and nice.[45] Such connotations among children find expression in their overt behavior toward objects of color. Psychiatrists Grier and Cobbs describe a relevant incident: "A black child was approached by a white child who rubbed his dark skin with her fingers and asked: 'But how do you ever get clean?' "[46] In his study of the connotations of color names, John E. Williams states that "an abundance of informal evidence can be offered to support the observation that, in our culture, the word (and color) black carries a negative or 'bad' connotative meaning, while the word white carries a positive or 'good' meaning."[47] He hypothesized that both blacks and Caucasians would differentiate significantly between the connotative meanings of black and white, with white being viewed more positively than black. "The study revealed that both Caucasian and Negro subjects perceived the color name white as significantly more positive in evaluative meaning than the color name black."[48] Although both groups differentiated between the terms on a significant level, the black group marked the term "black" as less negative than did the white group of subjects.

Color terms thus play an important role in the language of racism. Although we have concentrated on the color connotations of the terms "black" and "white," it should be noted that our language also encompasses the ever-threatening "yellow peril" and "red menace."

Color connotations are not the only examples of the racism embedded in our language. Terms that whites employ to "put down" nonwhites, to define a subjugated position for nonwhites, are also racist, even though they are frequently employed on an unconscious level. The use of such terms as "kid" and "boy" when referring to adult nonwhites causes great fury in interracial interaction. Bosmajian describes the reaction of the famous baseball player Elvin Hayes when a white reporter called him "boy": "Boy's on Tarzan. Boy plays on Trazan. I'm no boy. I'm 22 years old. I worked hard to become a man. I don't call you a boy."[49] Though the reporter protested that he meant nothing by the remark, his motivations cannot temper the impact of such terms on those at whom they are directed. Any language that, through a conscious or an unconscious attempt by the user, places a particular racial or ethnic group in an inferior position is racist at base and is almost certain to produce bristle responses highly disruptive to interracial communication.

Finally, an example of an insidiously racist use of language is the tendency of language users constantly to set people apart, to identify persons not as people, but as white people, black people, Japanese people, and so on.[50] At times, such language usage can be viewed as simply informative, a description of the objects in a scene. But within a racist context, this kind of specification works to the disadvantage of the object of description. The tendency to identify nonwhites who have excelled by their race, in a phrase such as "a great Negro ball player," represents almost an obsession with the identification of race. The hidden assumption that many nonwhites infer from such statements is that the white speaker really means, "He is a great ball player for a Negro"; that is, that it is somehow extraordinary for a black to be a great anything, and on those occasions where a black does excel, one must point out that it is rare indeed. The language of racism is also used to set racial and ethnic groups apart when they have done something "bad." Up until a very recent attempt by the mass media to refrain from this type of racial and ethnic identification, news reports almost always identified a criminal by race, if he was other than white. Bosmajian insists that this kind of selective identification of race through language is harmful to race relations:

If we were told, day in and day out, that "a *white* bank clerk embezzled" or "a *white* service station operator stole," it would make a difference in the same sense that it makes a difference to identify the criminal suspect as "Negro" or "black."[51]

Effects of Racist Language in Interracial Settings

As we suggested in Chapter 2, the victims of racist language have become sensitized to such expression and bristle at its usage. Racist language employed in the interracial communication setting produces: (1) anger and hostility toward the user of the language, (2) a keen distrust of the user, and (3) a reinforcement of all the negative stereotypes the victims of racist language hold of the user of such language. An individual who employs racist language may be unaware that his expressions are racist or that they are being perceived as racist by nonwhite receivers. Whites have been culturally conditioned to accept certain forms of expression and see nothing wrong in the employment of these cliché language patterns. By persisting in saying such things as "Negros" and "colored," they demonstrate ignorance and/or insensitivity toward the desire of nonwhites to redefine themselves and have their own terms accepted within the society. As Bosmajian suggests, changing language habits is in effect relinquishing the power of definition and the control of communication situations; the white communicator may not consciously wish to give up such an advantage.

Most of the contemporary racist language employed publicly is not so extreme and obvious as was the case with the white woman who tried to discourage Richard Wright from a career in writing: "You'll never be a writer," she said. "Who on earth put such ideas into your nigger head?"[52] The racism in language such as that expressed in words like "nigger," "kike," "jap," "chink," and "spic" is so obvious that they are seldom heard any longer in polite circles and especially not in interracial encounters in the more urban settings. More common today is the subtle racism in language. A refusal on the part of whites to say "black" instead of "colored," an insistence on the term "Mexican" rather than "chicano," and a constant reference to various nonwhite groups as "you people" are all interpreted by nonwhites in interracial settings as indications of racist attitudes on the part of the white language user.

Bosmajian states:

The Negroes' increased understanding and sensitivity to language as it is related to them demands that white Americans follow suit with a similar understanding and sensitivity which they have not yet demonstrated too well.[53]

Such a process of white language sensitization is easy to prescribe but difficult to carry out, because even a presumably "sensitized" white man like Bosmajian still persists in using the term "Negro," even when talking about the desire of "blacks" to define themselves. While he doubtless meant nothing by it, he himself cautions that such excuses are no longer applicable to interracial interaction:

In a few cases, a very few cases, white Americans indeed "didn't mean anything by it." That excuse, however, will no longer do. The whites must make a serious conscious effort to discard the racist clichés of the past, the overt and covert language of racism. "Free, white, and 21" or "that's white of you" are phrases that whites can no longer indulge in. . . .[54]

The importance of the disruptive qualities of such apparently innocent remarks in interracial communication must not be underestimated. Jack Daniel, in a study of interracial communication variables, asked groups of black subjects to list experiences with whites which upset them and interfered with interracial communication. Many of the experiences listed were cases where whites, knowingly or unknowingly, used racist expressions such as "you people," "little colored girl," "kid," and "boy."

The language of racism, be it obvious or subtle, is thus an enormous deterrent to effective interracial communication. As nonwhites become more sensitized to the racism inherent in white language usage and to the power of self-definition, white communicators will be placed under even more pressure to change their linguistic habits if productive interracial interaction is to proceed. It is never easy to voluntarily relinquish power, but when the exercise of that power has consistently produced deleterious effects in interracial settings, the value of simple pragmatism should dictate a change. Racist language habits of whites who wish to communicate effectively with nonwhites must be inhibited not only because it is morally correct to do so but also because racial tensions will not decrease until such a linguistic transformation has occurred.

It should be remembered, of course, that the elimination of racist language will not erase racist attitudes inherent in language users. Bringing racist expressions out into the open, however, and exposing them as racist elements will enable white speakers to identify more readily those habits that they may unconsciously possess and will sensitize them to terms that produce hostile effects in nonwhite listeners. Whereas the elimination of racist language will certainly not eliminate racism in this generation of language users, it may diminish the impact such language may have in shaping the racial attitudes of future generations of language users.

The process whereby white communicators may become sensitized to the language of racism and change their language habit patterns is difficult. Engaging in frequent and candid interracial interactions with nonwhites who will tell the white communicator which expressions cause bristle responses is one means of sensitizing oneself. Another less direct and less effective process by which one can inform oneself of the language patterns acceptable to nonwhites in interracial settings is through reading literature of various racial and ethnic movements. In this way one can become aware of the development of racial and ethnic thought and philosophy, particularly regarding the concept of self-definition.

The process of sensitization to language is also painful. Whites who speak candidly in interracial settings constantly risk being called racists and are frequently called on to examine motives and profound feelings and attitudes. Many whites object vehemently to the process, calling it racist and discriminatory in itself. "Why," they say, "do I have to be so careful and so sensitive to *them*? This is the way I have always spoken. Why can't they be just as sensitive to me? Why do I have to take this abuse?" These questions are relevant and meaningful and are difficult to answer to the comfort and satisfaction of the white communicator who is reluctant to effect a linguistic metamorphosis. Many whites claim that they become so "up-tight" and so conscious of offending that they can no longer communicate at all for fear of producing hostile reactions. In the initial phases of the sensitization process, this inhibition is common. It is a "hit or miss" game, and when they miss, they are negatively reinforced. The only way to approach this change in language patterns is as an educational experience, one that will enable an individual to grow in interracial understanding. At this point the change is "the white man's burden," for it has been the language of *white* racism that has perpetuated racist attitudes and caused the defensive racist language of nonwhites. As one engages in more frequent interracial interactions and develops more benign forms of expression to replace racist habits, interracial communication becomes less emotional, less painful, less hostile, and, consequently, much more productive.

CONTRACULTURAL LANGUAGE CODES

The language of white racism, expressions that set nondominant groups apart, degrade them, and control them through enforced definition, creates a reaction on the part of the victims of such language. The physical principle that "for every action there is an equal and opposite reaction" applies to this important social phenomenon. Racial and ethnic hostility expressed in racist language employed by a dominant society inevitably results in hostile feelings on the part of the oppressed. In Chapter 4 we discussed the development of countercultures as a reaction to the values and standards of the dominant culture. A frequent occurrence within a counterculture is the development of a contracultural language code, a means of expression that serves both to express hostile reactions and to preserve the integrity of the group. Another term that commonly refers to such a language code is "argot." Argot is viewed as a special type of linguistic code. Edith Folb defines it as follows: "These particular characteristics—usage limited to a particular group or class, secrecy, and usage associate with members outside the dominant culture—form the basis for the definition of argot."[55] Malcolm's hustler at the beginning of the chapter was speaking to Malcolm in argot; hence the non-Harlemite listener could not understand the code of the ghetto. It was secret, known only among black ghetto residents and most certainly differed from the language codes employed by the dominant culture. Although we shall concentrate on the argot of the racial countercultures in our society, it should be remembered that many other types of countercultures develop argot, for example, criminals, teenagers, the drug culture, homosexuals, and even labor movements.

Functions of Argot

In her comparative study of urban black argot, Folb outlines the several functions a secret code, or argot, performs for the counterculture.[56] First, argot aids the counterculture in providing a means of self-defense. For members of a subculture or counterculture to survive in a basically hostile environment, they must have a means of communicating with each other which cannot be understood or detected by the hostile forces at work against them. As Maurer states, "There must be threat from the dominant culture."[57] If threat from outside sources does not exist, the motivation for the development of a secret code is diminished, and argot does not develop beyond an elementary stage.

An outstanding example of the way in which argot is developed in the presence of threat as a means of self-defense is provided by the historical plight of the Jews in Spain during the time of the Inquisition. After the Arabs were defeated by Ferdinand and Isabella, the golden age of religious tolerance in Spain came to an end, and non-Christians were persecuted. They were given a choice by the Church of converting to Christianity or leaving the country. Many Jews left Spain rather than submit to Christianity and took the Spanish language with them to North Africa and other Mediterranean countries. They used Spanish in Greece, Turkey, and Italy as a code language through which they kept the Jewish culture alive. Other Jews, not wishing to leave Spain, remained and pretended to convert to Christianity. They secretly remained Jews, however. The language of Judeo-Spanish (ladino), a medieval form of Spanish with a considerable Hebrew influence, was developed. Ladino served as a code by which Spanish Jews could communicate with each other while excluding non-Jewish Spaniards.[58]

Eastern and middle European Jews also developed a code language and employed it in those areas where they were regarded as an "out-culture" and suffered discrimination and persecution. The code of Yiddish, a language derived from German, links Jews throughout Europe. Jews from Russia, Poland, Germany, Latvia, and Hungary could identify each other through the use of Yiddish and at the same time maintain a secrecy and security from the hostile dominant culture. Some Jews, in fact, living in European ghettos were so confined to their own out-group that they spoke only Yiddish and were not proficient in the language of the country in which they lived.

Many groups in this country also feel the need to defend themselves against a hostile dominant culture, and they have developed codes that are unique and differ greatly from the standards of the dominant culture. In the southwestern United States, the pachucos, a counterculture arising from the subculture of Mexican Americans, developed an argot of youth which draws from Mexican and American slang. The black population of this country, of course, has developed a refined language code that enables them to communicate with each other while maintaining a secrecy from the dominant society. As Grier states: "The indirectness of southern language patterns suited the needs of the oppressed black minority perfectly. In the circumlocution so necessary to the beleaguered blacks, it became a refined art."[59] Julius Lester describes how a secret language code serves as a means of self-defense for a subculture and/or counterculture:

Of the minority groups in this country, blacks are the only ones having no language of their own. Language serves to insulate a group and protect it from outsiders. Lacking this strong protection, black people are more victims of assimilation than the Puerto Rican, Italian, or Jew who can remove himself from America with one sentence in his native tongue.[60]

A second function of argot lies in its capacity to serve as a cultural storehouse for the hostility the counterculture feels toward the dominant culture. A secret code enables its users to express a felt hatred toward the dominant culture without members of the more powerful group detecting such expressions and punishing the user of the code. According to Grier, "the 'jive' language and the 'hip' language, while presented in a way that whites look upon simply as a quaint ethnic peculiarity, is used as a secret language to communicate hostility of blacks for whites, and great delight is taken by blacks when whites are confounded by the language."[61] Grier even suggests that the "Negro" spirituals so commonly sung within the dominant culture are actually filled with a duplicity of meaning through which slaves communicated to each other their plans to escape and expressed their feelings of hostility and rebellion against their condition.[62] Maurer points out that even the argot of the now almost-accepted labor movement was full of terms that expressed great hostility for nonlabor holdouts: "Such words as scab, strikebreaker, company man, and goon were once powerfully hostile words which helped labor organize in the United States. . . ."[63] Folb, in her lexicon of black argot, presents a series of words that black ghetto residents use to refer to whites; all are hostile expressions: "beast," "honky," "paddy," "pecker-wood," "devil," and "the man."[64] The Yiddish argot is also filled with words that refer to non-Jews in a highly pejorative way: words like 'goyim" and "schutzim" and expressions such as "it's too good for the 'goyim' " express the deep hostility that Jews feel toward the non-Jews whom they regard as oppressors. These secret codes thus provide a means by which society's out-groups can express their frustration and hatred without risking negative sanctions from the dominant society.

Finally, argot functions as a means of maintaining the identity and group solidarity of a subculture or counterculture. It enables the group members to identify each other and outsiders, and at the same time, outsiders can identify group members. As Lindgren suggests: "Of all the forms of social interaction, the language people speak is the most compelling and enduring source of cultural identity. Cultural identities and differences tend to follow linguistic lines."[65] Maurer emphasizes how such a secret code works to preserve a counterculture: "This threat intensifies the internal forces already at work and the argot forming there emphasizes the values, attitudes, and techniques of the sub-culture, at the same time downgrading or disparaging those of the dominant culture."[66] The development of argot represents a will toward self-identification, a drive to survive culturally with a unique integrity despite pressures from the outside dominant society to conform. Like the Jews in Spain, members of countercultures employing secret language codes exhibit a determination to survive on their own terms. As Folb says, "one's knowledge of argot presupposes a *conscious* attempt to actively identify oneself with a given group."

The Dynamics of Argot

Argot exists as long as those employing it feel they are threatened somehow by outside forces. As long as such a fear of the dominant society exists, members employing argot are motivated to keep their language code secret and exclusive to their group.

Maurer suggests that the escape of argot into general usage in the dominant society is a signal of the demise of the out-group culture that once employed it so exclusively:

When large numbers of words escape from the sub-culture, this is an indication of weakening hostility and the widespread diffusion of the sub-culture through friendly contacts with the dominant culture, which in turn means that the assimilation of the sub-culture is under way. This assimilation is usually preceded by a high rate of turnover in the vocabulary of the sub-culture, and followed by the gradual deterioration of the sub-culture.[67]

Understanding the effects of a breakdown of the secrecy of a code on the existence of an out-group culture explains why most countercultures are so possessive of their argot. Argot is an out-group cultural preservative, and, as it becomes coopted by the dominant group, the culture itself becomes ripe for extinction.

Examples of Contracultural Language Codes

Created under conditions of extreme stress and threat, contracultural language codes are frequently highly inventive and fascinating to study as examples of creativity involved in the attempts of certain out-groups to preserve and maintain their culture. Concentrating on black subcultures of urban ghettos, Edith Folb found in her research that "race predominated over economics or geography in the sharing of argot."[68] Black subjects living up to 10 miles apart in a large urban center were able to identify the same elements of meaning in their contracultural code.

In her analysis of the black urban lexicon, Folb divides her terms into eleven categories: (1) drugs, (2) acts of toughness, (3) verbal and physical forms of manipulation, (4) generalized physical activity, (5) material possessions, (6) personal appearance, (7) food and alcohol, (8) sex and sex-related acts, (9) interpersonal relations and personal names, (10) outsiders, and (11) miscellany.[69] The terms she presents related to drug activities represent a need of those employing such terms to protect themselves from the legal forces of the dominant culture by creating special words to stand for illegal acts and possessions. "Gunny," "skoofer," and "stencil" are marijuana items; "blunts" and "fender benders" are pills. To those outside this culture these terms have no particularly drug-related meanings.[70] Another interesting set of Folb's contracultural terms deals with various forms of manipulation. Certain linguistic authorities believe that black subcultures and countercultures employ language in a much more manipulative fashion than do whites. Folb presents under this category "those physical, verbal and material demonstrations on the part of one individual that have as their prime end the manipulation, advantage taking or showing up of another person."[71] "To fiend (or fonk) on someone" is to show someone up, particularly in your car, "to style" is to show off what you have, and "to bogart something" is to take more than your share of something.[72] Another category which Folb presents, that of "outsiders," has special meaning for interracial communication. This category refers to "expressions of racial derision [that] are generally 'in-house,' to be used by the black community out of earshot of the persons or class of people they deride."[73] It should be remembered that these expressions represent enormous feelings of interracial hostility. DeCoy, in his *Nigger Bible,* presents even more hostile words that contracultural black argot offers for the white man: "Alabaster Peers," "Mr. Charlie," "Miss Anne," and "The Great White Father." DeCoy employs these terms as "pertaining to that aspect of the Caucasian power structure, administrators, philosophers, government officials, social organizers, and theologians who exemplify and dictate what niggers live up to, emulate, and worship."[74]

Pachuco, as mentioned before, is another counterculture which has developed a self-defensive argot. According to Barker, "Pachuco is an argot of youth which borrows heavily from Mexican and American slang."[75] This group rejects both the Mexican and American groups and seeks to form a society of its own. Popular in the 1940s and 1950s as a criminal counterculture, "the pachuco has consistently and thoroughly resisted all attempts at his Americanization. . . ."[76] According to Braddy, an authority on pachuco argot, this counterculture did not contribute much as a protest movement or even, as is commonly asserted, in setting the styles of youth dress and fashions; the pachucos' main contribution, however, was in their language, which is derived mainly from Spanish and has an English influence. Like black argot, the argot of the pachucos, who lived primarily in the southwestern United States near the Mexican border, has many words for drugs and drug peddling: *"Camello"* (from Camel cigarettes, a term for a marijuana cigarette), *"cargo blanco"* (white cargo, or shipment of cocaine or morphine), *"submarino"* (submarine or yellow barbiturate pill). Because the pachucos engaged in many smuggling activities, they have in their argot several words to describe these illegal acts: a *"pildoro"* is a smuggler of pills, and *"trompeta,"* literally a trumpet in Spanish, denotes an informer. One of the most interesting aspects of pachuco argot is the manner in which users have incorporated English words into their Spanish-sounding language code: *"Ay te huacho* [watch]" is an expression for "I'll be seeing you"; *"bute alerta ese"* means "better watch yourself," *"bunche"* is "a lot," *"calam asu"* refers to a railroad, and *"watcho"* means "I watch."[77]

Even the Nisei, that "successful" nonwhite group that we normally regard as a subculture rather than a revolutionary counterculture, have code terms that are taken from the Japanese language but are applied to life in America and reflect the values of America as opposed to those of Japan. Words, for example, that are basically neutral in connotation in Japan take on racial overtones when used by the Nisei in the United States. As Stanford Lyman points out, the Nisei are too polite to say such things as Jew, white man, or nigger.[78] They realize these are touchy subjects in this country; in order to alienate no one and still enable themselves to express racial attitudes in language, they employ certain Japanese words as euphemisms. To refer to a white man, the Nisei use the terms *"hakujen"* (literally a white man), or the pejorative *"keto"* (hairy person or barbarian). In reference to blacks:

The Nisei, who combine a culturally derived mild antipathy to blackness with an unevenly experienced and ambivalent form of American prejudice, never employ racist language like coon, nigger, etc. Rather, they use the denotatively pejorative *Kuran-bo,* literally "black boy," usually in a neutral and unpejorative sense, at least on the conscious level.[79]

Japanese ambivalence toward the Chinese is reflected in the Nisei use of the Hawaiian term for Chinese (*pakē*), which also has certain minor negative connotations. One of the most creative expressions used by the Nisei is that which refers to "Jew." Lyman refers to the creation of this term as a "trans-Pacific linguistic transmogrification."[80] Anti-Semitism is almost unknown in Japan, but when the Nisei learned the special European-derived anti-Jewish sentiment, they invented a cleverly disguised means of referring to one central idea of the Jewish stereotype. Much too polite to ever employ the word "kike," the Nisei invented the neologism *"ku-ichi,"* which is not so much a reference to Jews as it is to the quality of stingyness. The term *"ku-ichi"* is a combination of the word *"ku,"* which is the Japanese word for the number nine, and *"ichi,"* which is the Japanese word for the number one. Nine plus one equals ten, and the word for ten in Japanese is *"ju,"* a homonym for the English word "Jew." The term *"ku-ichi"* is definitely argot, because, as a Nisei innovation, its meaning is not known in Japan. In Japan, the denotative word for "Jew" is *"yudaya-jin."*[81]

We have thus presented examples of black, pachuco, and Nisei argot that demonstrate the tendency on the part of out-group cultures to create secret language codes to protect the thoughts and actions of group members from the gaze and negative sanctions of the dominant society. The secrecy and hostility inherent in the existence of such contracultural language codes present obvious but nevertheless strong barriers to effective interracial communication.

Impact of Contracultural Codes on Interracial Communication

A primary problem in interracial communication can be traced to the historical communication relationship between whites and nonwhites in this country. Lewit and Abner present this relationship:

Communication between dominator and dominated tends to be limited to the dominator's instructions or demonstrations regarding desired work and cues for starting or changing work outlines, the dominated person's indication of compliance, the dominator's sanction of the work behavior, and their mutual confirmation of dominance in interpersonal roles . . . The development of communication for accommodation or genuine co-operation is neglected.[82]

Two languages thus develop on the part of the dominated; one is used in the presence of the dominator and one in the natural and comfortable environment where the dominated lives with others like him. "We may assume that blacks who live partly in a black world and partly in a white dominated world develop a dual language system of cues which activate one lexicon or the other.[83] Thus, according to Lewit and Abner, whereas many adult blacks, for example, may function linguistically in both worlds, some young blacks may not have developed language systems that enable them to accomplish this difficult task; they have difficulty understanding whites because they have a limited knowledge of the white lexicon and/or problems with their switching systems. Whites, of course, although fully capable of communicating with other whites, have never really had to live in two worlds and hence have problems communicating with blacks to the extent that black meanings differ from white meanings. The greater the dissimilarity in language structure between a source and a receiver, the greater will be the likelihood that the encoder–decoder mechanism will function inaccurately.

Co-operation is possible when words mean the same to both white and black, but co-operation and trust may be reduced in spontaneous naturalistic situations if the interacting person hears familiar words but infers meanings different from those of the speaker.[84]

It is almost a cliché by now to note that when a black or a youth says "That's bad," and really means "That's good," confusion on the part of the white adult receiver results.

Four basic linguistic differences between racial and ethnic groups in this country (excluding the language of white racism) have an enormous impact on the ability of members of different groups to interact. The first difference has been suggested by our discussion of contracultural language codes. The development of an argot suggests that there exist actual differences in denotative meanings among racial and ethnic groups. Words are taken out of the general cultural code and made to stand for totally different referents. To a black, for example, a "beast" refers to a white man, and to a white man a "beast" is an unpleasant animal. The difficulty arises in interracial communication because, as in the case of Malcolm's hustler, the words appear to be the same in both the dominant cultural code and the contracultural code, yet the meanings are different. Because contracultural codes serve a self-defense function, the meaning of the terms are kept secret; because whites cannot break the code significantly, they frequently experience breakdown on an interracial level. As Maurer suggests:

In fact, we have more linguistic and anthropological data on obscure primitive cultures from the South Seas to the Cape of Good Hope than we have on our own micro-systems. Yet, the hostility between sub-cultures and the dominant culture continues to generate, especially in the urban centers, intracultural conflict which has an increasingly deleterious effect on the dominant culture itself.[85]

Another linguistic barrier to communication between the races arises from the disparity in connotative meanings that members of different races hold for certain terms. Whereas various denotative meanings may be shared (that is, communicators may have the same referent in mind for the same symbol), the connotations associated with the referents vary greatly because of the lack of shared experience between whites and nonwhites. A term that may elicit a positive experiential association for a member of one race may elicit a negative reaction from a member of another. Such differences in the semantic profiles of the races significantly decrease the accuracy of communication between races. A study conducted by Lewit and Abner compared black and white semantic differences and revealed that "blacks have a somewhat different system of connotative meanings from whites and that communication of meaning among whites or blacks is more accurate than between black and white."[86] The study demonstrated, for example, that for blacks:

"Mother" is more *soft, safe* and *relaxed* than for whites, "Next Year" is less *new* and *alive,* "TV" is more *good* and *safe,* "Girls" are less *danger-*

ous, "Father" is less *good* and more *safe,* "Police" are less *good* and more *dangerous,* and "God" is less *alive.*[87]

These semantic differences reveal a significant diversity of experience which the various races hold with regard to word referents. It is thus quite difficult in interracial communication to share experience accurately through the use of words.

A third linguistic barrier that strongly affects interracial communication is not based on the diversity of word meanings but on differences found in language pronunciation and grammar or dialect differences among races and ethnic groups. A study of such differences by Labov and others produced evidence demonstrating the existence of pronunciation and grammar differences between blacks and whites of equal socioeconomic status.[88] According to Lewit and Abner, "Black dialect tends to be preferred and sustained in family and neighborhood contexts where norms of interaction and conversation content differ from those of white potential co-workers."[89] Because not all nonwhites have the capacity or willingness to switch their patterns of pronunciation and grammar, and, because most whites are not well enough acquainted with nonwhite pronunciation patterns and grammar, this divergence provides another barrier to interracial communication.

A fourth linguistic barrier that diminishes the effectiveness of interracial interaction derives not from the differential qualities and characteristics of the language patterns themselves but from the diverse notions various races and ethnic groups have concerning the proper function and use of language. Thomas Kochman maintains that dominant and dominated cultures use language in different ways.[90] In the case of the United States, the dominant white culture uses and perceives language in a "traditional sense" as a method of giving information. Excepting the "I mean what I say" formula for linguistic interpretation, members of the dominant culture attach maximum credibility to what is expressed in language. The dominated culture, on the other hand, uses language in a traditional sense in which what is said is interpreted literally and also employs language in a manipulative manner, in which language is viewed opportunistically as a means of obtaining what one wants. "A history of survival forces you to look for expedients, take advantage of opportunities, and focus on what will and will not work."[91] In black argot words like "shucking," "jiving," "rapping," and "gripping" suggest this manipulative function of language and describe communication that should not be taken literally. According to Kochman, the manipulative use of language occurs when one is operating from an equal or lower status. People of higher status, who can be assertive because of their position of power, need not engage in manipulative linguistic behavior, and so "the saleslady in the department store who cannot order you to buy, flatters you. The life insurance salesman gives you the impression that you are going to die tomorrow."[92]

The dominant white culture does not employ this "gaming" function of language; all is taken quite literally. Within the dominated culture, on the other hand, members "have a mind-set that allows them to perceive such 'gaming' maneuvers and enjoy them when they are for play, appreciate them when they are for profit, and subvert them when the 'game' is being 'whupped on them.' "[93] Given this disparity in interracial views regarding the function of language, it is inevitable that breakdown should occur between members of various races who hold different rules for communication. Whites, for example, because they take most linguistic expression literally, tend to overreact to certain kinds of black rhetoric designed by blacks to be manipulative and taken as fact by whites. This disparity, says Kochman, is one of the reasons the Black Panthers are so hated and feared by the white community, for when the Panthers say "off Whitey" in an attempt to express a bravado position, whites respond as if the next black they see were going to attempt to kill them.

The U.S. State Department tends to recognize the various uses of language employed by other nations, but in general officials ignore the fact that our subcultures and countercultures employ language differently as well. When Chinese Communists growl their threats, the United States does not take the communication at face value but always attempts to analyze the ways in which the Chinese are attempting to manipulate a situation. When they need reports of the facts of a given incident in the Middle East, diplomats usually go to Israel for information rather than to the Arab countries, not only because Israel is regarded more as an ally but also because it is generally believed that Arabs use language metaphorically to achieve certain emotional effects. Yet, whereas these differences are recognized on an international level, they tend to be ignored on a subcultural and contracultural level within the United States. Such an ignorance of the disparity in language users among subcultures and countercultures is another cause of the frequent disasters occurring in interracial communication situations.[94]

Language poses a problem in interracial communication, then, because members of different racial and ethnic groups in this country lack shared denotative and connotative meanings, possess differences in grammar and pronunciation patterns, and employ different game rules for the use of language itself.

SUMMARY

The language of racism is not merely reflective of racist thought and attitude in the culture; its use also produces racist thought in those exposed to it and helps to shape certain forms of racist behavior. The victims of the language of racism have become sensitized to it, because the aggressiveness and hostility inherent in the language of racism produces a threatening environment for the subculture or counterculture that is the object of such language. Such a threatening environment results in a reaction on the part of the counterculture. Contracultural language codes or argots are developed in the face of this hostility; they serve both as a means of self-defense, enabling the dominated culture to maintain its own unique identity, and also as a kind of reverse language of racism, which allows the victims in the dominated culture to express hostility toward those regarded as oppressors. Because the essence of the code is secrecy, users are able to express hostility illusively. The end result of this aggression–reaction cycle is possible communication breakdown on several levels:

1. The language of racism causes extreme emotional response in the objects of such language, which greatly inhibits further interaction.
2. The contracultural language code, as secret argot, becomes almost a foreign language. If the nonwhite member who employs the code is "bilingual," he may be able to speak within a white linguistic framework and also within the pattern defined by his own subculture or counterculture. He is thus able to communicate with whites on a "formal" level. If he speaks only in contracultural code, however, he may not have the tools to communicate on an interracial level at all. Because whites are prohibited from knowing the code, there is no way that they can become "bilingual" for the sake of interracial communication.

The solutions to the far-reaching problem that linguistic hostility and diversity inject into the interracial setting are multiple. First, the use of the language of white racism must be eliminated, for, as Bosmajian suggests, whites who want to interact on an interracial level in a productive fashion must become as sensitive to their offensive racist expressions as nonwhites have become. Members of the dominant society must engage in a very difficult modification of their personal linguistic habits.

The problem introduced into the interracial communication situation by the existence of contracultural codes is equally difficult to solve. If it were possible, if the dominant society could and would stop all discrimination against its subcultures and counter-cultures and establish friendly relationships with all racial and ethnic groups, then, according to Maurer, hostility between dominated cultures and the dominant cultures would decrease with such a diminution of ill feeling that the necessity of counter-cultures and contracultural codes would also decrease. The existing codes would become known to the general culture and hence would cease to function as a means of dividing people.

The development of such a utopian civilization is rather unlikely, in the near future at least, and many subcultures and counter-cultures are now beyond the point of desiring any form of assimilation. In a withdrawal phase, many want to maintain an identity apart from the dominant culture and consequently they desire to maintain their native languages and argot. What frequently begins as a reaction to cultural and racial discrimination develops into a strong cultural movement that may then persist long after the threat that gave rise to the movement is removed. Nonwhite users of argot, then, are not about to teach white members of the dominant culture their unique language code; such an action would be self-defeating in an environment that still remains hostile and threatening to members of racial and ethnic subcultures and countercultures.

From a white perspective then, one cannot attempt to master contracultural argot in order to engage in effective interracial communication. Nonwhites desiring interaction with whites must undoubtedly do what they always have done; that is, they will have to become proficient in two forms of linguistic expression, one to be used in communicating with whites and one to be used in communicating with members of other subcultures and countercultures. This "bilingual obligation" of nonwhites is mandatory in interracial communication only because the white culture is still the dominant culture. As such, language customs of white culture will be the linguistic standard imposed on the general community until or unless the power center shifts to another group. Thus if a nonwhite wishes to interact with the power center in any way, he most probably will have to use the language dictated by that center if he is to be understood. Malcolm X was extraordinarily "bilingual," for when he spoke to a white audience, his linguistic patterns were clear and comfortable to his white listeners and he was able to make himself clearly understood. When he spoke to a black audience, it was equally clear that, through his command of black linguistic patterns, he was an integral part of the black community.

The "bilingual obligation" may seem a heavy burden to impose on the nonwhite segments of our society, but because countercultures resent attempts by whites to use argot and perceive such attempts as efforts to strip the counterculture of identity, the burden seems almost self-imposed. Ideally the dominant society should not have everything on its own terms, even though it holds the power, for the persistent resistance of the counterculture will eventually undermine that power. The obligation of the white community therefore, if interracial communication is to exist with any positive effect, is to respect the right and need of every racial and ethnic group in society to establish and maintain its own linguistic patterns. The ever-increasing research into the plausibility of actually teaching black dialects in ghetto schools and maintaining Spanish-speaking courses reflects the understanding of some educators of the desirability of developing the self-concept and self-worth of various groups by allowing them to preserve and perpetuate their own languages.

Regardless of the cultural desirability of maintaining linguistic diversity in our multicultural society, some common language patterns are obviously necessary for interracial communication to occur. Participants in interracial interaction must realize that members of different racial and ethnic groups have different language habits—different denotations, connotations, grammar, pronunciation, and concepts of the function of language. A sensitivity to such differences and a willingness to make the adjustments necessary for common understanding is a giant step toward resolving the difficulties resulting from linguistic diversity.

Activities

1. What expressions and jingles can you recall from your youth that used racist language as an essential element? What expressions do you consciously or unconsciously employ now that could be interpreted by a sensitized person as racist?
2. Have you ever employed or do you now employ any linguistic code that is outside the mainstream of general linguistic expression? When and why do you employ it?
3. Divide the class into racial groups. Any group that employs a special code should develop a brief sample lexicon of terms (e.g., black argot, chicano code, Yinglish/Yiddish, etc.). Discuss these terms in class to determine how many are truly secretive, that is, how many are unknown to members of other racial or ethnic groups. An interesting extension of this activity is to have the various groups in the class exchange lists and take the "strange" terms into their own communities to see how well such a code has remained secret.
4. What terms for any argot—drug, youth, racial, etc.—can you think of which began as a secret code designed for self-protection and which now have become part of the parlance of the general culture? What phenomenon might have produced this "leakage"?

NOTES

1. Malcolm X, *The Autobiography of Malcolm X* (New York: Grove, 1965), p. 315. Reprinted by permission of Grove Press, Inc. Copyright 1965 by Alex Haley and Malcolm X; copyright 1965 by Alex Haley and Betty Shabazz.
2. Edward Sapir, *Language: An Introduction to the Study of Speech* (New York: Harcourt Brace Jovanovich, 1920), p. 7.
3. George A. Miller, "Psycholinguistics," in *Handbook of Social Psychology,* ed. Gardner Kindzey (Reading, Mass.: Addison-Wesley, 1956), p. 693.
4. Ibid.
5. Margaret Schaluch, *The Gift of Language* (New York: Dover, 1955), p. 11.
6. Joseph A. DeVito, *The Psychology of Speech and Language: An*

Introduction to Psycholinguistics (New York: Random House, 1970), p. 7.

7. Ibid.
8. Walter Lippmann, *Public Opinion* (New York: Macmillan, 1957), p. 54.
9. DeVito, op cit., p. 199.
10. Ibid.
11. Jerome S. Bruner, "The Course of Cognitive Growth," *Amer. Psychol.* 19 (1964): 1–15.
12. Lyman Bryson, "Problems of Communication," *The Communication of Ideas, a Series of Addresses,* ed. Lyman Bryson (New York: Cooper Square, 1964), p. 3.
13. Stuart Chase, *The Tyranny of Words* (New York: Harcourt Brace Jovanovich, 1938), p. 63.
14. Hubert Alexander, *Language and Thinking: A Philosophical Introduction* (New York: Van Nostrand Reinhold, 1967), p. 23.
15. DeVito, op. cit., p. 203.
16. Ibid.
17. Alexander, op. cit., p. 22.
18. DeVito, op. cit., pp. 204–205.
19. Ibid.
20. Harry Hoijer, "Language and Writing," in *Man, Culture, and Society,* ed. Harry L. Shapiro (New York: Oxford University Press, 1960), pp. 196–223.
21. DeVito, op. cit., p. 203.
22. Ibid.
23. Ibid., p. 201: and Schaluch, op. cit., p. 261.
24. DeVito, op. cit.
25. Hoijer, op. cit., p. 196.
26. Charles E. Osgood and Thomas A. Sebeck, *Psycholinguistics: A Survey of Theory and Research,* with A. Richard Diebold, Jr., *A Survey of Psycholinguistic Research, 1954–1964* (Bloomington, Ind.: Indiana University Press, 1965), p. 194.
27. Hoijer, op. cit., p. 3.
28. Bryson, op. cit., p. 3.
29. Simon Podair, "Language and Prejudice Toward Negroes," *Phylon* 17 (1956): 390.
30. James P. Coner, "White Racism; Its Root, Form, Function," *Amer. J. Psychiat.* 126, no. 6 (1969): 805.
31. Haig Bosmajian, "The Magic Word in Nazi Persuasion," in *The Language of Suppression* (Encino, Calif.: Dickenson, in press), p. 9.

32. Lerone Bennett, Jr., "What's in a Name?" *EBONY Magazine* (November, 1967). Reprinted by permission of *EBONY Magazine.* Copyright 1967 by Johnson Publishing Company, Inc.

33. Harold Isaacs, *The New World of Negro Americans* (New York: John Day, 1963), p. 84.

34. Haig Bosmajian, "The Language of White Racism," *College English* 31 (December 1969): 264.

35. Ibid.

36. Podair, op. cit., p. 390.

37. Bosmajian, "White Racism," p. 267.

38. Bennett, op. cit., p. 411.

39. S. I. Hayakawa, *Language in Thought and Action* (New York: Harcourt Brace Jovanovich, 1963), p. 226.

40. Isaacs, op. cit. pp. 74–75.

41. William Blake, "The Little Black Boy," *The Norton Anthology of English Literature,* Vol. III (New York: Norton, 1962), p. 51.

42. Bosmajian, "White Racism," p. 265.

43. Podair, op cit., p. 392.

44. Bosmajian, "White Racism," p. 267.

45. Mary Ellen Goodman, *Race Awareness in Young Children* (New York: Collier, 1964), p. 130.

46. William Grier and Price M. Cobbs, *Black Rage* (New York: Basic Books, 1968), p. 134.

47. John E. Williams, "Connotations of Color Names Among Negroes and Caucasians," *Percept. Mot. Skills* 18 (1964): 721.

48. Ibid., p. 729.

49. Bosmajian, "White Racism," p. 268.

50. Ibid., p. 270.

51. Ibid., p. 271.

52. Richard Wright, *Black Boy* (New York: Harper & Row, 1966), p. 162.

53. Bosmajian, "White Racism," p. 267.

54. Ibid., p. 271.

55. Edith A. Folb, "A Comparative Study of Urban Black Argot," *Occasional Papers in Linguistics,* no. 1, UCLA (1972): 10.

56. Ibid., pp. 10–11.

57. David W. Maurer, "Linguistic Hostility as a Factor in Intra-Cultural Conflict," *Actes du Dixième Congrès des Linguistes* (Bucharest: Éditions de L'Académie de la République Socialiste de Roumanie, 1969).

58. Henry Clay Lindgren, *An Introduction to Social Psychology* (New York: Wiley, 1969), p. 228.

59. Grier and Cobbs, op. cit., p. 124.

60. Julius Lester, *Look Out Whitey! Black Power's Gon' Get Your Mama!* (New York: Grove, 1968), p. 90.
61. Grier and Cobbs, op. cit., p. 124.
62. Ibid., p. 123.
63. Maurer, op. cit., p. 1.
64. Folb, op. cit., pp. 107–109.
65. Lindgren, op. cit., p. 228.
66. Maurer, op. cit., p. 4.
67. Ibid., p. 6.
68. Folb, op. cit., p. 1.
69. Ibid., p. 87.
70. Ibid., p. 89.
71. Ibid., p. 94.
72. Ibid., pp. 94–95.
73. Ibid., p. 109.
74. Robert deCoy, *The Beginning Point Commencing a Series of Works Toward Creation of the Nigger Bible* (Los Angeles: Holloway House, 1967), p. 29.
75. George C. Barker, "Social Functions of Language in a Mexican-American Community," *Acta Americana* 5 (1947): 193.
76. Haldeen Braddy, "The Pachucos and Their Argot," *Southern Folklore Quarterly* 24 (1960): 263.
77. Ibid., pp. 255–271.
78. Stanford Lyman, "Generation and Character: The Case of the Japanese Americans," in *The Asian in the West* (Reno, Nevada: Desert Research Institute, Western Studies Center, University of Nevada System).
79. Ibid.
80. Ibid.
81. Ibid., p. 53.
82. David Lewit and Edward Abner, "Black-White Semantic Differences and Interracial Communication," *J. App. Psychol.* 1, no. 3 (1971): 276.
83. Ibid., p. 266.
84. Ibid., p. 264.
85. Maurer, op. cit., p. 7.
86. Lewit and Abner, op. cit., p. 276.
87. Ibid., p. 270.
88. William Labov, Paul Cohen, and Clarence Robins, "A Preliminary Study of the Structure of English Used by Negro and Puerto Rican

Speakers in New York City," *Cooperative Research Project No. 3091* (New York: Columbia University Press, 1965).

89. Lewit and Abner, op. cit., p. 265.
90. Thomas Kochman, "Cross-Cultural Communication: Contrasting Perspectives, Conflicting Sensibilities" (Unpublished paper, Chicago, Northwestern Illinois State College, July 1970), pp. 43–44.
91. Ibid., p. 43.
92. Ibid., p. 44.
93. Ibid., p. 45.
94. Ibid.

7

Interracial Implications of
Nonverbal Communication

Much communication that takes place between members of different racial and ethnic groups is nonverbal. The importance of nonverbal communication in interracial settings is even more evident than in racially homogeneous settings because in the United States basic geographical and psychological separation of the races has made it difficult for them to get close enough together to communicate verbally. Because of this segregation much interracial communication has occurred with communicators sending nonverbal messages. Nonverbal communication is significant in interracial settings not only because of this physical separation of the races but also because (as was demonstrated in the chapter on beliefs, attitudes, and values) the lack of trust among the races has caused interracial communicators to reject the face values of verbal communication and to search for nonverbal cues as indicators of real meaning and response in interracial communication situations.

Interracial Significance of Nonverbal Communication

As Barnlund suggests: "Differences of time and place, changes in dress, posture, or facial expression modify and sometimes totally override the literal meaning of a message."[1] We tend to regard nonverbal communication as the "true" indicator of a communicator's meaning, because nonverbal behavior (frequently unconscious or reflexive) is more difficult to control than verbal behavior. The "true self" seems to be revealed more readily in nonverbal than in verbal ways.

Sapir acknowledged the importance of the nonverbal forms of communication as early as 1927: "We respond to gestures with an extreme alertness and, one might say, in accordance with an elaborate and secret code that is written nowhere, known by none, and understood by all."[2] The notion of some form of universal non-

verbal expression that all, regardless of race or nation, can understand has intrigued many researchers. Jurgen Duesch suggests
that nonverbal communication is the main form of interracial communication:

Nonverbal denotation is used as an international, intercultural, interracial,
and interspecies language; it is adapted to communication with an out-
group. Verbal denotation is used as a culturally specific language; it is
adapted to communication with the in-group.[3]

How such a cross-cultural universally understood form of expression can exist is explained by Mehrabian:

How it is possible that, despite the absence of any explicitly accepted
standards as to what certain behaviors mean, people are still able to
understand each other's nonverbal communication? . . . To resolve
this puzzle, we must remember that people rarely transmit nonverbally
the kinds of complex information that they can convey with words.
Nonverbal behavior primarily involves the communication of one's feelings
and attitudes, and these are rather simply described.[4]

The question of whether certain nonverbal communications are
universal in meaning is controversial. There are those who maintain that such gestural expression is not universal, that the meaning of nonverbal acts can be grossly misinterpreted across
cultures. These same researchers suggest that such physical
forms of expression, far from being instinctual to all men, are
culturally determined. Weston Labarre,[5] in his crosscultural
study of certain physical expressions of emotion, maintains
that the expression of emotion in one culture is open to serious
misinterpretation in another. He claims that there is no "natural"
language of emotional gesture; gestures mean opposite things in
various cultures. For example, hissing in Japan is regarded as a
polite expression of deference to a superior; the Basato culture
means hissing to stand for applause; and in England hissing is regarded as a rude disapprobation of an actor. Spitting in many cultures is symbolic of contempt, but in the African Masai tribe it indicates affection and benediction; in certain American Indian
tribes spitting is employed as a method of healing by a medicine
man. To urinate on another in Occidental societies is a gross in-
sult; in certain African communities the same act is seen as a
positive transfer of power by the medicine man. All this evidence,
according to Labarre, is indicative of the lack of universality of

nonverbal expression and the importance that culture plays in determining the meaning of gestural forms of expression.

Paul Secord also sought to demonstrate the impact of culture on the interpretation of meaning in nonverbal communication.[6] In his study, subjects studied photographs and formed impressions. The experimenter attempted to determine the cultural factors that contributed to impression formation. He found that culture did in fact determine the meaning of certain nonverbal cues. For example, the amount of lipstick worn in our culture made a greater impact on the impressions projected to the subjects than did the shape of the ears of the photographed person. The culture provided ready-made categories consisting of denotative cues and associated personality attributes such as those associated with age and sex roles or racial and ethnic stereotypes.

Ray L. Birdwhistell, a pioneer in the study of nonverbal communication, asserts a compromise view regarding this nonverbal universality controversy. According to Birdwhistell, smiling across cultures is a universal gesture; all humans seem to do it, but that smile may have a different significance within different cultures. Meaning, thus, must be studied within a specific cultural context (intrachannel) and not from the denotative point of view of another culture.

Following along this same line of research, Ekman and Friesen, in a cross-cultural descriptive study, attempted to discern if facial and emotional expressions are a universal primitive response that crosses the barriers between literate and illiterate cultures.[7] The data were gathered in New Guinea, where subjects were told a story and then asked to identify a picture that revealed the appropriate emotion of the story. The results indicated that certain facial behaviors are universally associated with particular emotions.

There do seem to be, then, certain universal nonverbal expressions of emotion; there is also ample evidence to indicate strong cultural variations in terms of what a given gesture or expression denotes. The assumption that all nonverbal communication is universal in meaning could lead to serious intercultural misunderstandings.

Dimensions of Nonverbal Communication

Nonverbal communication is very important in interracial situations, for even when verbal communication breaks down or ceases, nonverbal communication continues. Nonverbal communication refers to all forms of expression that are not linguistically based. In the remainder of this chapter we shall include the following variables as components of nonverbal communication and examine the manner in which these variables facilitate and/or disrupt interracial interaction.

1. Environment   This dimension includes those external factors that affect interaction, especially interracial interaction. The major divisions of this aspect of nonverbal communication are: (1) general ambience, which includes climate, population density, and aesthetic surroundings, and (2) proxemics, which can be viewed as the use of "social and personal space and Man's perception of it."[8]

2. Communicator appearance   This dimension includes considerations of both the communicator's personal style of attire and his unique physical characteristics.

3. Nonverbal behavior   Included in this dimension are all non-linguistically based acts that serve as communication stimuli. Specifically this dimension includes: (1) kinesics, which encompasses the study of body movement, posture, and facial expression, and (2) paralanguage, which refers to nonlanguage sounds, vocal qualities, pronunciation, and inflection patterns.

ENVIRONMENT

General Ambience

Among the most overlooked of . . . factors in communication are those that arise from the setting in which interaction occurs. Cues that originate in the natural environment unaltered by Man or from the environment he has created exert an influence upon behavior that is only vaguely sensed.[9]

Authorities concerned with race relations dread the onset of the hot summer months for the impatience and hostility they evoke among those living in crowded conditions of urban ghettos. The relationship between racial conflict and summer heat waves is evident. Some experimental documentation supports the notion

that climate very much affects the manner in which people interact.

Griffith and Veitch hypothesized that "interpersonal attraction
responses and subjective evaluations of affective feelings are more
negative under conditions of high effective temperature than under
conditions of normal effective temperature, and more negative
under conditions of high population density than in low density
conditions."[10] Their study confirmed this. Such findings help to
explain why urban ghetto conditions, with a lack of heat in winter
and air conditioning in summer, contribute to the negative feelings
reflected in the interracial interaction that ensues, particularly that
between police force members and urban dwellers. Ambience in
the form of temperature and population density no doubt has an
enormous impact on interaction.

The above study dealt with general interpersonal interaction
and not specifically with interracial interaction. The subjects did
not have necessarily negative feelings toward each other before
the experiment. In interracial settings, for the most part, the participants already possess some negative affective attraction. Ambience becomes even more critical in interracial settings, then,
because an uncomfortable environment will increase the already
explosive nature of the setting. Examples, of course, are the Harlem, Detroit, Chicago, and Watts riots of the mid-1960s.

Aesthetic Stimulation
"Men, like plants and animals, draw upon their environment for
sustenance, and may be impoverished or enriched by it."[11] The
architect is more important in terms of social interaction than most
would expect, for, consciously or unconsciously, people are very
much guided and moved by the objects and forms that surround
them. As the famous architect Eero Saarinen stated:

. . . the influence of the room is stronger than our character and our
character is improved or depraved, depending on whether the room is
esthetically—or why not say "ethically"—on a higher or lower level than
we ourselves.[12]

Experimental studies have demonstrated that aesthetic surroundings affect the frame of mind and sense of well-being of an
individual and hence influence his interaction. Maslow and Mintz
placed subjects in beautiful, average, and ugly rooms and asked

them to rate photographs of faces in terms of fatigue and energy, of displeasure and well-being.[13] Subjects in the beautiful rooms gave significantly higher scores; that is, they perceived the pictures as reflecting more energy and well-being. The subjects in the average rooms had the next highest scores, whereas the subjects in the ugly rooms actually perceived displeasure and fatigue in the same pictures. In a follow-up study Mintz examined the experimenters of the previous research. Those who had spent time interviewing in the beautiful room were compared with those who had interviewed in the ugly room. Those in the ugly rooms finished their interviews more quickly, experienced monotony, fatigue, headaches, discontent, irritability, hostility, and an avoidance response to the room. Those interviewers who had worked in the beautiful room experienced comfort, pleasure, enjoyment, energy, and a desire to continue the activity.[14] Thus the aesthetic environment does have an impact on individuals within that environment.

Implications of Environment for Interracial Communication

The environment in which communication occurs, including factors of climate, population density, and aesthetic appeal, guides the direction and intensity of interaction. In situations where diversity in roles, beliefs, attitudes, values, perceptions, and language already complicate the communication process (as in interracial settings), a negative environment will increase the impact of that diversity and lead toward the expression of interracial hostility. The street corner of an urban ghetto on a hot summer night is probably not the most conducive setting for open and fruitful interracial communication.

An analysis of the comparative environments of the various races in this country gives some insight into the differential perceptions, attitudes, and affective responses of interracial communicators. Hot (or cold) overcrowded conditions such as those found in many poverty areas, coupled with unpleasant aesthetic surroundings, develop negative predispositions and perceptions in those subjected to such conditions and help to contribute to interracial hostility. Certain whites from middle-class neighborhoods have a "rosier" perception of the world based on the input of a different physical environment. This disparity of physical environments, which results in different mind sets, causes many problems in interracial communication.

This is not to suggest that all nonwhites live under poverty conditions. A significant and unfortunate number do, however, and one cause of the failure of interracial communication is the social force creating the physical conditions; this in turn creates the psychological conditions prohibitive to interracial interaction. There are, of course, intraracial communication problems resulting from a disparity in physical surroundings. Many middle- and upper-class nonwhites, coming from physical environments different than those of certain ghetto dwellers, experience communication breakdown with members of their own race because of the divergence in the psychological set determined by the ambience in which they find themselves. The same can be said of the communication experienced by whites of various social classes and different geographical neighborhoods. Those who physically leave economically depressed areas cannot help leaving such areas psychologically as well; the impact of environment on thinking and perception processes is strong.

Proxemics

Proximity, interaction, and friendship   Proxemics refers to the study of "social and personal space and Man's perception of it."[15] A specific area of concentration within proxemics is the relationship between proximity, interaction, and friendship. One theory of "integration" as a means of solving racial problems advances that proximity leads to interaction which in turn leads to the development of interracial friendship. The results of several studies lend support to this theory.

Merton found in his study of a housing project that the majority of friends lived across from each other, that is, within basic sight lines. When the subjects lived side-by-side in a court setting, they did not develop as many friendships because interaction was more difficult.[16] Whyte, in a three-and-a-half-year study of street gangs, found that the individual member's place of residence entirely determined his interaction with others for the rest of his life.[17] Rosenfeld's experiment attempted to determine whether interpersonal proximity is used as an instrumental act for the attainment of social approval. Female subjects were assigned approval-seeking or approval-avoidance roles and were compared on the basis of their subsequent proximity to a female confederate in an otherwise unstructured social situation. The approval-seeking subjects positioned themselves significantly closer to the confederate. Individuals thus seeking friendship also seek proximity.[18]

Physician Abraham White conducted an informal experiment in which he attempted to determine whether removing the desk as a barrier between doctor and patient would have any effect on the way in which patients conducted themselves in an interview. He found that with the desk removed, 55.4 percent of the patients sat "at ease." With the desk in place, only 10.8 percent manifested relaxed positions.[19] In another study dealing with proximity and its effect on interaction, Sommer and Ross found that geriatric patients were not interacting in a new ward because the chairs were placed against the wall. When the furniture was rearranged in circles or around tables, there was considerably more interaction.[20]

The findings and theories of proxemics and interaction have been applied to the study of interracial interaction. Ernest Works comments on his extensive research in this area:

Research conducted among white tenants in integrated and segregated housing projects validate what may be called a general prejudice-interaction hypothesis, that out-group prejudice is reduced through intimate group contacts of those equal in status. This study investigates the hypothesis from the point of view of the Negro; that anti-white prejudice is diminished through intimate and interracial contact of persons equal in status. Our data in general supports this hypothesis.[21]

Albert Mehrabian comments further on the same phenomenon:

Some of the classical prejudice studies have shown also that housing projects that permit people of different races to live in close proximity lessen their prejudice toward one another . . . If increased contact can reduce negative (prejudiced) feelings and even convert them to positive ones, then its effect should be even more profound in cases where the initial attitudes are neutral, as would be the case with two strangers.[22]

Mehrabian also points out, however, the one important exception to this generalization: When hostile groups of persons are placed in close proximity, the increased contact and interaction does not necessarily improve their relationship.

Thus with the exception of cases of extreme hostility, the evidence points to the significance of interracial communication (brought about by increased interracial proximity) as a means of reducing interracial conflict and increasing interracial friendships.

Physical segregation precludes interaction and hence inhibits any chance of reconciliation and mutual understanding between the races.

Personal space   Another concept within the area of proxemics is that of "personal space." Personal space can be viewed "as territory that is carried around with the individual having invisible boundaries. . . ."[23] People have very definite concepts regarding personal space and propriety of behavior. Normal persons, for example, usually sit at corner angles when interacting; schizophrenics choose distant positions, separating themselves from each other by objects such as chairs. Females usually sit closer to females than they do to males.[24] As Barnlund suggests, "Every individual, with guidance from his culture, also develops a sense of personal space, the distance at which he prefers to interact with others."[25] As anyone who has traveled extensively will recall, certain cultures dictate that he should speak in a position very close to the receiver. Our culture suggests a pattern of interaction in which the communicators remain about 2 to 3 feet from each other; when a member of another culture speaks closer to us, we feel uneasy. "Marked differences in spatial styles, then, may cause the same message uttered from various distances to be assigned different meanings and motives."[26] When the sense of personal space is violated during communication, orientation toward the fellow communicator is likely to be modified.

The concept of personal space is of great importance in interracial communication settings. Society's taboo against interracial sexual contact, coupled with the many sexual stereotypes associated with various races, makes personal space more important in interracial communication than in most interpersonal contact. Researcher Grace Halsell claims that sex is at the base of racism. The theory she advances is that "the white male's fear of the black male's sexual prowess has been exaggerated out of all proportion. . . ."[27] Historically, of course, this syndrome is traced back to the slave period in which white men raped black women, thus creating the fear in themselves that, if given the chance, black men would seek revenge by raping white women. According to Berkeley historian Winthrop D. Jordon:

In our minds interracial sex is not so much a shared activity as it is a dangerous, reprehensible yet fascinating scene of raw lust between "a white" and "a Negro." Lust: we find it hard to think that it could be anything else, anything so personal as love and affection.[28]

Thus, whereas rape is regarded everywhere in the community as an undesirable and ugly offense, interracial rape is viewed in some areas as a capital crime.

This societal taboo against interracial physical mingling, together with interracial sexual stereotypes, has created interesting physical behavior patterns between the races in communication situations. A "touch–don't touch" phenomenon has developed, which is strongly tied to the stereotype held by whites that blacks and other nonwhites are unclean and have unpleasant odors and textures. Such a physical stereotype explains the strong physical avoidance patterns demonstrated in interracial settings. One black member of an interracial encounter group described his perception of the physical reaction of white women when he sits next to them on buses. The black man reenacted the subtle but observable physical withdrawal of a white woman as she moved ever so close to the window and fixed her eyes in a stare outward so she would not have to confront the black male face to face. In an episode of *All in the Family,* Archie Bunker exemplifies this physical avoidance response when he is so uncomfortably hesitant about drinking out of the same glass from which Sammy Davis, Jr., has also drunk, although he seems to have no reservation about drinking out of the same glass that his white neighbor has used. In the same episode Archie expresses his surprise and disdain on seeing black and white celebrities kissing each other on television. Thus when Sammy Davis kisses Archie at the end of the show, the audience roars with laughter, for they understand that Archie's sense of personal space has been violated.

The "touch–don't touch" phenomenon is a conflict that is characteristically experienced by the white "liberal" who wishes to overcome the physical contact taboo in order to demonstrate overtly his lack of racism. Such a white liberal communicator frequently develops a "touch compulsion," in which he feels compelled to clasp eagerly the hand of a new black acquaintance or to take a bite casually from a black colleague's sandwich. This compulsion becomes evident when the "touching" moves are overdone, when the white is engaged in more hand clasping and embracing with nonwhites than he would normally engage in with whites. In a sense it might be advanced that the white communicator is "protesting too much," that his compulsion to touch is really an attempt on his part to overcome his own strong aversion to touching members of nonwhite racial groups.

The concept of "touch" is thus an enormously strong and subtle force in interracial contact. Sexual myths have imposed taboos on interracial physical contact, and these barriers are based on conscious and unconscious fears and a basic ignorance of the physical features of other racial groups. In interracial settings, attempts to maintain a strong sense of personal space are greater than in ordinary communication settings. The keen awareness of personal space results in self-consciousness and an underlying physical tension which, though subtle, is nevertheless extremely disruptive and serves as one cause of ensuing breakdowns in verbal communication.

The occupation of territory This dimension of proxemics is related to personal space, but it embraces a broader physical domain. "The concept of territoriality goes beyond 'staking out' a piece of land for oneself. People possess areas, such as desks, favorite chairs, rooms that are not to be intruded upon, or even particular seats at the eating table."[29] Thus, even the smallest child in a family soon learns his proper seat for eating and the areas in which he may play. Animals stake out territories for themselves; if overcrowding causes others to invade staked-out territories, fighting occurs. Chombart de Lauvre found that in France, when the number of people living in a particular dwelling reaches the condition where there are fewer than 8 to 10 square meters for each individual, physical conflict and social problems double.[30]

Being in one's own territory during the time of any confrontation gives the individual an advantage. According to Mehrabian, "an animal who fights in his own territory almost invariably wins":[31]

A man's home is his castle, and a person is indeed "boss" in his own territory. The psychological advantage that he has within his own territory is lost to his host when he goes visiting elsewhere. The higher a person's status, the greater is the area he can claim as his territory and therefore the greater is the likelihood that he will retain his psychological advantage in dealing with others. So, we have a two sided relationship; people of high status claim and regulate access to larger territories and those who already have access to larger territories are able thereby to assume the advantage of higher status.[32]

The occupation of territory has significant implications for interracial communication. It was no accident that much time was spent searching for neutral ground to hold peace negotiations between North Viet Nam and the United States. In order to diminish the territorial advantage of either party, a nonpartisan communication setting had to be found. The same need obtains for interracial communication situations. Territorial considerations explain much interracial conflict. The white society occupies most of the territory in the United States, particularly the most "desirable" territory; hence whites enjoy a higher status. That territory occupied by nonwhites, because it is comparatively so small, is held jealously by its occupants, and any attempt to usurp it is met with extreme hostility. The Black Panthers, for example, view the police as an "invading force," comparable to a hostile foreign army. By this definition they justify resisting the police as a means of protecting and fighting for the "homeland." White social workers in the ghetto also violate nonwhite territory. Their questions and interviews, conducted within nonwhite homes, though mandatory for the welfare bureaucracy, are viewed as invasions of privacy. Further, white "volunteers" who think they are being socially constructive by "going into the ghetto to raise them to our standards" are also enormously resented, for they are coopting already occupied territory. In interracial encounters the subjects of police, social workers, and white community and charity volunteers are extremely volatile, for they represent a threat to the status that accompanies the occupation of one's own territory.

COMMUNICATOR APPEARANCE

Not only does our general ambience act to determine the course of much of our communication, but our personal appearance, the image we project, also plays an important role. The impression we give through the manner in which we are physically perceived by others communicates to our receivers without necessitating any verbal communication from us and helps determine how others in turn will communicate toward us.

Clothing
By clothing we mean all personal apparel and decoration that individuals choose for themselves. Some contend that one's selections in clothing are accurate reflections of his personality, that a

conservative style of dress, for example, suggests a conservative personality. Barnlund suggests: "Dress may also be a way of giving tangible expression to one's self concept. There is a belief in retail and advertising circles that clothing, jewelry, personal articles, even automobiles and houses are bought mainly to project a desired image."[33]

In an experiment studying the relationship of dress to certain personality measures, Aiken had female subjects answer opinion questionnaires regarding clothing and compared the results with a personality analysis. He found that those who favored strong decoration exhibited uncomplicated socially oriented personalities; those who liked comfort in clothing were controlled extroverts; subjects manifesting an interest in dress seemed socially conscientious but insecure; those preferring conformity in dress codes also emphasized social, economic, and religious values; and subjects who opted for economy in dress exhibited signs of responsibility, conscientiousness, alertness, efficiency, and control.[34]

Whether dress habits and preferences really do reflect personality traits is not the crucial question. What is important is that individuals tend to perceive dress patterns as indicators of personality traits. We respond to dress as if it were an accurate projection of an individual's character; that is, we stereotype people according to the clothes they wear.

Studies of how social judgments are formed suggest that appraisals of others are made effortlessly and with little conscious awareness. In a few seconds, the perceiver gains enough information from a visual inspection of posture, face, hands, and clothing to form a clear image of the other person and to guide his own responses to him.[35]

Barnlund further states, "If a consistent relationship between character and apparel is sustained by further research, taste in clothing could give reliable clues to the traits of others and be used to anticipate their behavior."[36] Mary Shaw Ryan, in a study in which subjects were asked to attribute personality traits to models wearing certain types of clothes, found that subjects attribute like traits to models dressed similarly and different traits to models in different attire. She determined that clothes definitely influence the impressions of character and personality projected by those we meet. Clothes were also judged to be indicative of the mood of the individual attired; the manner in which a person is dressed is seen as an indicator of what he is planning to do next. According to Ryan:

We have found that clothes do play a part, often an important part, in the way we perceive an individual. Clothes may give us clues as to the sex, age, occupation, socio-economic status, organizations to which the individual belongs, material attitudes, and personalities of the subject. For some characteristics, our perceptions have a high degree of accuracy, but for others, such as personality characteristics, that accuracy may not be much more valid than chance opinion. The perception of certain characteristics determined by certain attributes of garments may be the same for all observers, others are similar for specific groups, while others are individually determined.[37]

In another study of the impact of dress on the perception of personality traits, girls who did not wear lipstick were rated for various personality attributes. The results indicated a stereotype of girls who use lipstick, particularly regarding the following traits: They were seen as frivolous rather than serious, talkative rather than silent, and were said to have a marked interest in the opposite sex.[38] Lefkowitz and others conducted a fascinating experiment in which clothing was related to status and influence. Subjects were put in the position of following the example of a confederate. Subjects in the experiment violated stop signals more often in the presence of a confederate who led in the signal violations than when there was no confederate or the confederate conformed to the dictates of the signal. Significantly more violations occurred among subjects when the confederate who disobeyed the signal was dressed to represent high-status social groups. The study demonstrated that we tend to pick well-dressed persons as our leaders (if that is the value of our culture), and we will even follow them though illegal actions as if their style of dress legitimatizes the offense.[39]

A final study that demonstrates the manner in which we stereotype based on physical appearance was conducted by Thornton. Subjects were asked to judge pictures of individuals with and without glasses; those with glasses were chosen as more intelligent, industrious, honest, and dependable.[40]

As suggested in the chapter on roles and culture, clothing is one way in which sub- and countercultures distinguish themselves from the larger dominant culture. These clothing variations may sometimes be regarded as an act of rebellion, as in the case of the refusal of the "hippie" cult to conform to the dress standards of the more conventional society; on the other hand, such divergence in dress may simply be a manifestation of a subcultural pattern, such as in the case of the American Indian dressed in ritual garb. Differences in dress habits are both racial and socioeconomic. The Black Muslims, for example, dress in a simple conservative garb as opposed to the more extravagant costume of a ghetto hustler. The pachuco contributed his own dress style, which became personified in the "leather jacket" look of the 1950s. The dress styles of social classes differ according to the kind of attire they can afford.

Dress patterns and the stereotypes associated with them have an important impact on interracial communication. Nonconformity to the dress code of the dominant culture is frequently met with scorn on the part of "establishment" members. One need only note the hostility with which many members of the older generation regard the long-haired youth with bare feet and wrinkled war-surplus-type uniforms. Such contracultural dress patterns meet the most resistance, hostility, and distrust from establishment types, because such patterns constitute a symbolic rejection of the values of the dominant culture and a refusal to be controlled by it. The black emphasis on African dress style, for example, demonstrates both a rejection of dominant cultural values and a search for a cultural rebirth stemming from a new and different source than the dominant white culture.

Dress and grooming patterns constitute one of the strongest and easiest bases for stereotyping. A black with an Afro hair style, for example, is automatically labeled a "militant" by certain segments of the society. That hair style comes to suggest an entire series of beliefs, attitudes, and values to the perceiver, which may be positive or negative depending on the values of the perceiver. From the point of view of many in the dominant culture, a youth with long hair, dirty jeans, and no shoes is obviously a drug addict; this assumption is made with no further evidence than dress patterns to support it. Conversely, from the point of view of the contracultural member, a white man with a crew cut and a coat and tie is automatically classified as "establishment."

Working as they do, stereotypes create tendencies to perceive selectively; thus a white person who has stereotyped a black who happens to be wearing an Afro as militant will undoubtedly see only those things suggesting a militant posture; in this manner, the stereotype will be reinforced.

Clothing, then, while it may provide us with some information about a person, also tends to block input of other information by causing us to perceive selectively based on our stereotype of clothing patterns and personality types. In order to overcome this effect, communicators must engage in a dedicated effort to fight consciously the impact of these preconceptions about clothing. One of the best examples of the effect clothing has on communicators is the way in which uniforms effect people. To the wearer of a uniform, this manner of dress provides anonymity, power in the numbers of others wearing identical uniforms, and lack of personal responsibility for action. As the military has well demonstrated, a uniform can perhaps effect a change in a person in order for him to carry out orders. This dehumanization can explain how and why young men could shoot students at Kent State University or massacre civilians at My Lai. To the perceiver, the uniformed person is also seen as unhuman. The uniform removes from view any unique qualities that distinguish the wearer as an individual. With that style of dress, the wearer becomes a symbol of authority and power. Depending on the attitude of the perceiver regarding that power and authority, the presence of the uniform may elicit uncritical obedience or uncontrolled rebellion. In either case the style of dress totally diminishes the significance of the individual wearing the uniform.

The above is an extreme case in which clothing conditions our perception of the individual. Given this strong impulse to stereotype and thus dehumanize, those in interracial communication situations must attempt to suspend clothing judgments and probe beneath the external appearance of the other communicators.

Physical Characteristics

Communicators not only stereotype on the basis of what others wear in terms of clothing and personal decoration. They also form stereotypes based on actual physical characteristics of those interacting. Culture dictates certain standards of beauty and those physical traits deemed desirable; thus members of a culture respond to the physical makeup of each other in the pattern determined by the society. As Barnlund states:

The size and form of another person's body, along with the various positions it assumes, may affect the inferences we make about his attitudes and the way we interpret his words. . . . Whether warranted or not, the existence of such physical stereotypes will necessarily affect interpersonal perceptions.[41]

Our perceptions and interactions are very much influenced by these physical stereotypes. In our society, for example, height, in a male, is highly valued and seen as a source of pride. Height suggests power and strength. On the other hand, height in a female, because of society's role definition of the sexes, is viewed negatively. An overly tall woman is seen as a misfit, in much the same way as is a short man. Stereotypes regarding height in this country demand that to "be normal," a woman should be small and diminutive and appear to need protection and dominance of her tall mate-hero.

Much research has been conducted to demonstrate that individuals tend to link physical traits with personality traits. Wells and Siegal conducted an experiment in which subjects were shown silhouettes of three basic body types and asked to rate them in terms of personality. The heavy short figure was seen as older, old-fashioned, less good-looking, more talkative, less strong, warm-hearted, sympathetic, good-natured, agreeable, dependable, and trusting. The tall well-built figure (in terms of the aesthetic values of our culture) was perceived as strong, masculine, good-looking, adventurous, young, mature, and self-reliant. Finally, the tall thin figure was described as young, ambitious, suspicious, tense, nervous, less maculine, stubborn, difficult, pessimistic, and quiet.[42] The results of a study such as this point to the very strong influence our perception of physical traits has on our view of a person's character.

Secord, Dukes, and Bevan conducted further research into the impact of physical traits on perception of character traits. Subjects were asked to describe certain perceived facial characteristics that they observed in twenty-four photographs and to ascribe personality traits to the subjects of the photographs. Those who were described as extreme in physical appearance were also given extreme personality characteristics. The significant traits chosen were age, skin texture, fullness of lips, and facial tension.[43]

Secord and others conducted another experiment, this time

focusing on racial characteristics. They hypothesized that "there is no difference in the degree of personality stereotyping of Negro photographs varying widely in physiognomic Negroidness. That is, even if he has a Caucasian-like appearance, a Negro will be seen as having in full degree all the stereotyped traits usually attributed to the Negro."[44] Evidence from the experiment supported this hypothesis: "The generally accepted but seldom tested definition of a stereotype as a categorical response to a member of a minority group is thus upheld."[45] In this study researchers also hypothesized that "anti-Negro judges exaggerate the personality stereotype of Negroes, whereas pro-Negro judges de-emphasize it."[46] The experimental results lend significant support to this hypothesis.

Thus physical traits, specifically racial characteristics, provide fuel for personality stereotyping. In our society physical standards of beauty, that which is defined as "beautiful," "attractive," and "desirable," have traditionally been defined through advertising and the media by the dominant white community. Those imbued with such "white" standards of attractiveness frequently experience a type of physiological revulsion at what the white society defines as nonbeautiful. Standards of beauty are not absolute but are culturally induced, so that the tattooed face of an African native woman might be regarded as an exquisite specimen within its own milieu and be judged as nothing more than physical mutilation in this country.

A large part of the racist consciousness in the United States is the aesthetic definition of anything nonwhite as necessarily unattractive and therefore undesirable. Certain black features, for example, have been singled out as targets for disdain, such as hair, skin color, skin texture, nose, lips, and body scent. Racist language is filled with expressions of distaste for these black physical traits, for example, "nigger's wool," "liver lips," or "tar baby." This intense revulsion on the part of many whites to these nonwhite characteristics may be conscious or unconscious; it may be based on a physical fear of nonwhites or may be the product of a natural aversion toward that which is strange or different. Whatever the distinct cause, there is no question that this physical disdain is in part induced and reinforced by the dominant culture.

Much of the personal space orientation and touch aversion occurring in interracial communication settings is based on this physical revulsion and a fear of the unknown physical qualities so exaggerated and fabricated by racist myth. Absurd as it may seem, some whites even fear that somehow a close physical contact with a nonwhite will cause physical darkness to rub off on them. These complex physical avoidance patterns, especially on the part of whites toward nonwhites, are based on aesthetic standards, psychological fear, and conditioned physiological response. The problem is further complicated by the societal taboo that forbids races to come together closely enough so that these myths and fears can be erased.

The effect of this single standard of attractiveness and the physical revulsion demonstrated by whites regarding nonwhites is a tragic and crippling self-hatred on the part of those who are victimized. Before their contemporary efforts to develop their own standards of beauty and desirability, black men and women, attempting to contort themselves into the white man's image of attractiveness, engaged in the very painful process of "conking" their hair by undergoing an agonizing acid rinse in order to straighten and disguise their naturally curly hair. Malcolm X vividly describes this process and its psychological meaning in his autobiography:

The congolene just felt warm when Shorty started combing it. But then my head caught fire.

I gritted my teeth and tried to pull the sides of the kitchen table together. The comb felt as if it was raking my skin off.

My eyes watered, my nose was running. I couldn't stand it any longer; I bolted to the washbasin. I was cursing Shorty with every name I could think of when he got the spray going and started soap-lathering my head.

* * *

This was my first really big step toward self-degradation: when I endured all of that pain, literally burning my flesh with lye, in order to cook my natural hair until it was limp, to have it look like a white man's hair. I had joined that multitude of Negro men and women in America who are brainwashed into believing that the black people are "inferior"—and white people "superior"—that they will even violate and mutilate their God-created bodies to try to look "pretty" by white standards.[47]

Blacks are not the only group within our society who have suffered the indignity and self-hatred imposed by a single arbitrary standard of "white beauty." Many Jewish and Italian women, whose noses are larger than that prescribed by the white Anglo-Saxon Protestant value, undergo painful cosmetic surgery in order to make their features conform more to the standards dictated by the dominant culture. Even without regard to race, flat-chested women undergo various forms of cosmetic surgery hoping modern inventions in plastics will enable them to conform more readily to billboard images.

The issue of the existence of self-hatred among nonwhites as a result of the forced imposition of white aesthetic standards is extremely controversial, with many nonwhites denying this self-hatred hypothesis. In several interracial encounter groups conducted by this researcher, the question of negative self-concept among nonwhites was met with militant contradiction by many nonwhites, particularly those who were developing philosophies of nationalism and racial pride. Other nonwhites, attempting honestly and openly to assess their own responses to society's standards, admitted to experiencing certain feelings of self-deprecation at some time in their lives as a result of the white standards of beauty forced upon them and their inability to conform to those standards. The real issue seems to be not so much whether nonwhites actually experience self-hatred, but whether or not they should admit to such feelings in the presence of whites. Such admissions, according to many nonwhites, work against the movement toward racial dignity and self-sufficiency.

In attempting to present examples of such racial self-derision, this researcher requested permission to reprint a devastating poem by a Japanese American entitled "I Hate My Wife for Her Flat Yellow Face,"[48] in which the speaker of the poem painfully expresses his conflict in reconciling Oriental standards of beauty and culture with those of the white culture, personified ironically by a Jewish character, Judith Gluck. The poet, Ronald Tanaka, refused such permission, however, asserting that such conflicts in self-images should not be used by whites to over-romanticize and glamorize the self-hatred hypothesis. Regardless of the image nonwhites would like to project, however, evidence such as the sentiments revealed in Malcolm X's description of the painful "conking" process and, in fact, in the very title of Tanaka's poem point to the unpleasant conclusion that the imposition of negative physical stereotypes and white values on nonwhite races has an ego impact of some significance.

These negative physical stereotypes based on arbitrary standards of beauty are not immutable. As the taboos regarding interracial interaction break down, and they can and do, the physical stereotypes and attraction patterns change as well. Prior to World War II, for example, the Oriental, especially the Japanese, was severely stereotyped on the basis of certain physical traits deemed unattractive. He was described and projected in an exaggerated caricature as a "buck-toothed," "squinty-eyed" devil. After World War II, with American occupation forces in Japan, the physical space between Caucasian Americans and Japanese began to diminish, and some of the physical barriers were removed. Intermarriages took place, and new Japanese war brides had to be taken into American Caucasian homes. To effect this integration, a subtle redefinition of beauty began to take place in order to accommodate Oriental features and values. Caucasian women wanting to be in the vogue, began to shape their eyes in a "doe" fashion. (Ironically, and with reference to the previously discussed self-hatred, many war brides, wanting to adapt to Caucasian standards, underwent surgery to remove partially the epicanthic folds from their eyes in order more to resemble Caucasian women.) In the United States home decoration styles turned Oriental, and even dress styles tried to copy the mandarin and kimono mode of the Far East. The "China doll" image of the Oriental woman was a far cry from the "Uncle Tojo" stereotype of the prewar years.

Even today standards of attractiveness are changing. Nonwhites have begun to demand that the society recognize multiple standards of beauty. The "natural" hair styles and African garb worn by many blacks are succeeding in changing the white negative stereotype of black features. Some whites are even copying the black standards by allowing hair to grow into "natural" styles and wearing African-type clothing (to the dismay, incidentally, of many blacks who feel their movement is being coopted by such an overly zealous acceptance on the part of the white community).

Standards of physical beauty are thus culturally induced and change through time. Participants in interracial interaction, in order to overcome the physical barriers imposed by arbitrary standards of attractiveness, must begin to realize that previously all-white value patterns have been destructively chauvinistic. Like innocent children we need to rediscover others of different races; we must have the freedom to explore, to touch one another, to encounter real differences and significant similarities, to remove the mystery imposed by forced physical separation. If through interracial encounters we cannot break down these physical barriers, we shall be chained forever to the myths that cause us to run in fright from the unknown.

NONVERBAL BEHAVIOR

Much of our behavior, though not specifically linguistic, is nonetheless profoundly communicative. The way in which we move, our postural stance, our gestures and facial expressions, and our nonlinguistic vocal traits all communicate a message regarding our thoughts and intentions to receivers.

Kinesics

Definition of kinesics   According to pioneer Ray L. Birdwhistell, kinesics is "the systematic study of those patterned and learned aspects of body motion which can be demonstrated to have communicational value."[49] Birdwhistell asserts that emotional states are expressed through culturally determined nonverbal body sets that may be interpreted accurately within our culture but inaccurately in a foreign culture. In an experimental study Paul Ekman demonstrated that people can read emotional states through the observation of physical nonverbal behavior with considerable accuracy. Photographs and recordings of individuals in stressful and stress-release situations were shown to subjects. With considerable precision the subjects were able to match the verbal expression with the photographs of the emotional state. Although they were not able to distinguish the emotional state on the basis of the observation of the body alone, they could do so accurately when looking at either just the head and/or the head and the body positions. Physical behavior, then, can be interpreted accurately as a means of expressing human emotional states.[50]

Posture   Because postural communication is such an important, though subtle, form of nonverbal communication, much research has been conducted regarding the various functions different parts of the body serve in nonverbal communication. Different parts of the body have differing communicative attributes. In another study, for example, Ekman found that the head carries information about the particular affect experienced and relatively little about the intensity of the affect. Body cues suggest the level of arousal or intensity but tell us little about the particular affect being experienced.[51]

General body posture expresses much regarding the state of the individual. A study by James indicated that people can read the emotion signified by bodily postures. His subjects, observing photographs of a number of body postures, were asked to describe the expressive value of the position and to designate the particular emotion being communicated. The subjects were able to do so at a significant level of accuracy. It was further found in this study that the head and trunk positions are more basic to the communication than are the extremities.[52]

Albert Mehrabian discusses a specific posture and the expressive meaning it suggests: Regarding what he calls the "proxemic metaphor," he states:

A basic and transcultural element of human life is that people approach and get more involved with things they like, things that appeal to them, and they avoid things that do not appeal to them and that induce pain and fear.[53]

The approach/avoidance responses are basic postural patterns that express liking/disliking, security/fear, acceptance/rejection. The woman on the bus described by the black man in the encounter group session did not need to utter a word in order to express her dislike and rejection of this man when he sat next to her. Her subtle withdrawal as she inched toward the window expressed information regarding her emotional state and attitude.

Felix Deutsch suggests several other expressive postures. Tension postures, for example, body states that are derived from muscle tension or the release of such tension tend to reflect anxiety or its absence. Prohibiting and permissive postures reflected in the protected or open body positions suggest that the communicator is open to the gratification of pleasure or wishes to shield himself from such an experience.[54]

Mehrabian describes another posture, essential to understanding interracial interaction; termed the "power metaphor," this posture is expressed in terms of body expansion or contraction:

For the second dimension, dominance or status, the communication code seems to be based on a power or fearlessness metaphor. Power coexists with large size (for example, strutting versus shuffling, expansive versus small, and controlled postures and movements). Absence of fear (the opposite of vigilance) is implied by relaxation versus tension and by the ability to turn one's back to another.[55]

The implications of postural communication for interracial interaction are significant. The lack of trust between the races, the inability of individuals in interracial settings to "turn one's back to another," and the constant state of vigilance observed by participants are expressed in the extreme body tensions present in interracial situations. There is rarely the same degree of total body relaxation in interracial groups as there is in racially homogeneous groups.

Aside from the general posture of tension expressed in interracial settings, the social and sexual taboos that have maintained a relatively segregated society for so long frequently result in a physical and psychological fear and revulsion on the part of all the members of an interracial group. Fear and revulsion are expressed in avoidance postures, as individuals in interracial settings maintain a keen sense of personal space. The avoidance response is cyclical; as the source projects an avoidance message to the receiver, the receiver responds in kind.

Historical role definitions imposed by whites on nonwhites demanded that certain physical postures be assumed by nonwhites in the presence of whites. Given the "power metaphor," by forcing someone to "bow and scrape," one can demean him and strip him of all strength and influence. For many years in the South, for example, it was expected that blacks would physically lower themselves in the presence of whites and that they would always show deference by physically removing themselves from the white man's path. In the modern counterculture, a change in such posture signifies an overt defiance toward those traditional roles. Assuming an expansive size and a special walk enables members of the counterculture to assert their power and authority over their destinies.

Such physical moves can be volatile in terms of communication impact. In one interracial group discussion an elderly white man confessed that when he was driving and saw two young black men "strutting down the street," he became so angry he wanted to run them over with his automobile. So communicative was their physical action that these two pedestrians were able to elicit an extraordinarily violent response from a total stranger without ever saying a word to him or directing an action specifically toward him. Thus much of the tension and hostility felt in interracial settings is not verbally expressed but physically felt and behaviorally transmitted.

Gesture   Much interest among researchers has been manifested regarding the study of gesture as a form of nonverbal communication. In his study on muscle action Edwin Corbin maintains that such bodily action is a regressive substitute for verbalization. Muscle action is employed by the individual in place of words and represents a more primitive kind of communicative response than does verbal expression.[56] Allen Raskin in his study of gesture suggests that anxiety can be observed by muscle tautness and an excessive use of the hands.[57] An experimental study by Maurice Krout demonstrated that gestural symbolism for males and females differs.[58]

In his work *Gesture and Environment* David Efron began to study the gestural habits of certain selected ethnic groups. He observed the gestural patterns of eastern Jews and southern Italians living under similar and different environmental conditions in New York City. Efron found:

. . . gestural behavior, or the absence of it, is, to some extent, at least, conditioned by factors of a socio-psychological nature . . . They certainly do not bear out the contention that this form of behavior is determined by biological descent.[59]

To verify further the contention that gestural behavioral patterns are culturally induced rather than inherited, Efron found that members of ethnic groups that had been assimilated into the dominant culture demonstrated significantly less gestural behavior than did the members of ethnic groups that had remained within the domain of the traditions of the group.

In interracial settings gesture can reveal the same tension and hostility common to postural communication. Some spontaneous gestures in interracial settings, however, have become codified into a very keen symbolic form of expression. On October 16, 1968, for example, two black Olympic medal winners, while receiving their awards, raised black gloved fists and, with heads bowed, refused to salute the flag of their country (the United States). The clenched fist has become a symbol of defiance and can be found in revolutionary propaganda literature from that of the Black Panthers to messages from the Women's Liberation Movement. This one-time spontaneous gesture has grown into a nonverbal communication of specific significance. The *V* sign, once so familiarly employed by Winston Churchill as the sign of victory in World War II, has in this generation come to symbolize the contemporary struggle for peace. Such a gesture unites all those who use it with a common philosophical bond. The "secret" black handshake also unites members of one racial group in a common cause. This symbolic gesture systematically excludes those outside the racial and ethnic group in much the same way as does a contracultural language code. Gesture is thus also an important form of communication in interracial settings.

Eye contact   Love songs testify to the importance of the "eyes" in communication. "Your lips tell me 'No No,' but there's 'Yes Yes' in your eyes," is a simple but accurate way of explaining the way in which eye contact and expression can give the lie to verbal expression. The degree of eye contact maintained in interpersonal communication has been linked to personality traits and affective needs. Ralph Exline, for example, found that women seek more direct eye contact in interaction than do men and that those individuals with high affiliative tendencies need more direct eye contact. Conversely, competitive personalities seem to require less eye contact in interpersonal communication.[60] In another study Exline and others found that subjects looked at interviewers least when discussing personal subjects in an attempt to conceal personal information and feelings.[61] Efran and Broughton further found that individuals with high approval/dependence needs spend a great deal of time in direct eye contact with relevant others in interpersonal communication.[62]

Eye contact and expression plays an important role in communication between the races. The famous "glare" expressed so frequently by nonwhites toward whites presents in a moment the entire history of tension and hostility between the races. Such a glance, while mirroring the emotions of the nonwhite communicator, reinforces the feelings of fear and defensiveness in the white receiver. Communication in interracial settings is also often characterized by the actual avoidance of any type of eye contact, suggesting a dislike or distrust among the communicators. People tend to feel that another cannot lie if he is confronted face to face and that, if a communicator can engage in direct eye contact, he most probably has nothing to hide. Direct eye contact, then, must be considered as an essential ingredient in building positive interracial attitudes.

Facial expression   Research in nonverbal communication has also revealed that facial expression is a significant means of expressing emotions and attitudes. Frijda found that facial clues help to identify a general attitude of the communicator, and situational clues aid in specifying the emotion.[63] Vinacke further verified that knowledge of the situation affected the interpreter's judgment of the emotion communicated; he also found that Japanese, Chinese, and Caucasians display identical patterns of interpretation of facial expression but that they differ significantly in the degree of emotion perceived.[64] Zaidel and Mehrabian's experimental study verified the hypothesis that negative attitudes are more effectively communicated through facial expression than are positive attitudes.[65]

Studies have also been conducted to study various kinds of facial expressions and the meanings they relay. Frijda and Philipszoon, in a study in which subjects rated and analyzed facial expressions in photographs, obtained five factors of expressive meaning: pleasantness/unpleasantness, naturalness/artificiality, submission/condescension, intensity of expression/control of expression, and attentional activity/disinterest.[66] In a discussion of the meaning of various facial expressions, Sandor Feldman states:

The erect head expresses self esteem, self confidence, courage, looking ahead, health, stamina, pride, and strength. The bowed head expresses humility, resignation, guilt, and admission.[67]

Such a statement, reminiscent of the physical descriptions of the elocutionists, is superficial, because it draws vast attitude and personality implications from very slight expressive movements. Such an interpretation from a scholarly point of view is dangerous, because it does not account for individual expressive traits or situational variables. Feldman does provide us, however, through this type of analysis, with an excellent example of the degree to which people read meaning into facial expression, a meaning that may or may not be intended by the communicator.

The communication carried on through facial expression is important in interracial settings, because it reflects directly on the credibility of the communicators. We can lie verbally and consciously control what we say, but our physical behavior, especially our facial expressions, tends to mirror the reality within us. Erving Goffman refers to these two forms of communication:

The expressiveness of the individual (and therefore his capacity to give impressions) appears to involve two radically different kinds of sign-activity; the expression that he *gives,* and the expression that he *gives off.* The first involves verbal symbols or their substitutes which he uses admittedly and solely to convey information that he and others are known to attach to these symbols. This is communication in the traditional narrow sense. The second involves a wide range of action that others can treat as symptomatic of the actor, the expectation being that the action was performed for reasons other than the information conveyed in this way.[68]

We have less control over the impressions we "give off," because nonverbal behavior is more reflexive in nature. Understanding this, receivers of communication frequently—perhaps unconsciously—look at the body, the face, and the eyes of the communicator to discern the real intent and meaning of a communication message.

The studies cited previously demonstrate that we can interpret meaning from facial expression accurately, consistently, and, to some extent, cross-culturally. They also have shown that we are able to communicate negative attitudes more effectively than positive ones; we thus communicate hostility, tension, and irritation (so frequent in interracial communication) best of all. Unfortunately positive attitudes are not so well or vividly reflected in facial expressions. Given the common hostility inherent in so many interracial settings and the predisposition of individuals in interracial encounters selectively to perceive negativism, these negative facial expressions can come to dominate interracial interaction. Interracial communication can become stifled and strife-ridden through facial expression alone. Such explosive situations are frequently followed by laments such as "What did I say?" or "I didn't say anything!" The communicator may be correct in asserting that he said nothing *verbally,* but he undoubtedly said a great deal through a facial expression that could not be hidden.

Noncommittal facial expressions are not the answer to interracial communication problems resulting from nonverbal conflict. As Feldman suggests:

The noncommittal facial expression *is* an expression on the face; but *seemingly,* it betrays only that the person does not want anyone to know anything about his feelings. There is no *expression* on the face; a *lack of expression is the expression.* It is a "poker face."[69]

The only meaning that a facial expression such as this projects is that of uninvolvement and aloofness, hardly a remedy for interracial conflict.

Communicators in interracial settings must realize that in hostile or tense communication situations, persons are going to seek all avenues open for interpretation of meaning; these will include the selective observation of bodily and facial expression. Whether or not we verbalize our tensions and anxieties, our bodies express what our words may attempt to hide. Being aware of the communicative power of one's unconscious physical expression, communicators should be better able to deal with the difficulties that arise in interracial settings as a result of unspoken expressions of emotions and attitudes.

Paralanguage

Definition   "Simply put, paralanguage deals with how something is said and not what is said. It deals with the range of nonverbal cues surrounding common speech behavior."[70] Trager includes the following components as the constituents of paralanguage:

A. Vocal Qualities: (pitch, range, rhythm, tempo, articulation, etc.)
B. Vocalizations:
   1. Vocal characterizers: (laughing, crying, sighing, yawning, swallowing, etc.)
   2. Vocal qualifiers   (intensity, pitch heights, extent)
   3. Vocal segregates: ("uh huh," "um," "uh")[71]

Mahl and Shulze also include the following characteristics as part of paralanguage: dialect or accent, nonfluencies, speech rate, latency of response, duration of utterance, and interaction rates.[72]

Dialect/accent and interracial communication   Whereas all these factors of paralanguage are interesting aspects for communication study, the most relevant element in paralanguage in terms of interracial communication is the impact that accent or dialect patterns have upon communication receivers. Accents and dialects carry with them stereotypes of the speakers employing them, and these stereotypes affect interracial interaction. In an experimental study on accent Haines found that the vocal cues of grammar and pronunciation employed by certain members of the society serve as status cues. The higher the status assigned the individual, the more credible he was perceived to be; and accent also affects a speaker's credibility.[73] Wilke and Snyder tested students from different geographical areas. The subjects listened to recordings and were tested to determine their ability to identify the speaker's home and their attitudes toward the accent. The results showed a significant similarity of attitudes toward accents among subjects from different geographical locations. The general American dialect was the most preferred, and foreign and New York dialects were least preferred. Subjects were also able to accurately identify New York, Boston, southern, and foreign accents. Other accents were more difficult to identify.[74]

Anisfeld and others conducted an interesting experiment regarding vocal stereotypes based on accent cues. Gentile and Jewish college students were asked to evaluate personalities of recorded voices. Some of the voices employed general American accents and some had pronounced Jewish accents. The experimenters also correlated the results with the subjects' attitudes toward Jews. The accented voices in the study were devalued in terms of height, good looks, and leadership. The Gentile subjects did not consider the accented voices as more favorable with regard to any trait. The Jewish subjects favored the accented voices in terms of humor and kindness.[75]

In a similar study W. E. Lambert and others attempted to determine the vocal stereotypes that Canadian residents hold. English and French Canadians were asked to rank English and French speakers on height, good looks, leadership, humor, intelligence, religiousness, self-confidence, dependability, kindness, ambition, sociability, character, and likeability. The English subjects evaluated English speakers as more favorable on most traits. French subjects, surprisingly, also evaluated English speakers as more favorable than French speakers; they devalued the French speakers to an even greater degree than did the English raters.[76]

The interracial implications of vocal stereotypes are vast. Many nonwhites of the United States are not only physically stereotyped, but they are vocally stereotyped as well. Southern black speech, found in various forms all over the country, is negatively viewed by many whites. The speech patterns of chicanos, while speaking in English, are regarded as a foreign accent by many whites, in the same manner as the chicanos are regarded as foreigners. Even the Japanese are stereotyped vocally, as the studies in Chapter 3 suggest, with so many whites perceiving them primarily as soft-spoken. The standard of speech set forth by the white upper- and middle-class members of the society, exemplified daily by national newscasters and commentators, carries with it a status. Those who employ it are regarded by the dominant society as responsible and intelligent. Those who do not conform are regarded as illiterate and stupid.

Dialects and accents present two problems in interracial communication. First, they actually can disrupt information transfer among communicators when differences in speech patterns make mutual understanding impossible. The constant need to repeat oneself, to find other more easily pronounceable words, to speak more slowly and deliberately, along with the frustration of facing a lack of comprehension by the receiver, cause frustration and embarrassment on the part of the speaker and irritation and frustration on the part of the receiver. Simple differences in accent serve to compound the already significant differences in perceptions, beliefs, attitudes, values, role expectations, and language codes between various racial groups.

Second, negative vocal stereotyping of certain dialects and accents frequently causes a receiver to "turn off" a speaker, to disregard the content of a communicator's message before it has been received on the basis of the receiver's negative view of the manner in which the message is delivered. The communication problem in this situation is brought about by the impulse to be so busily engaged in stereotyping *how* a person says something that no time is spent in listening to *what* precisely has been said. Conditioned to believe that those with certain accents are unintelligent, the receiver frequently dismisses messages as "stupid"; the same messages might very well have been received positively if the same content been expressed in an accent more positively stereotyped. These stereotypic responses to accent and dialect must be overcome, of course, before communicators can succeed in going beyond the rudimentary stages of interracial contact.

CONCLUSION

Distance and segregation among the races in this country have caused much interracial communication to be nonverbal and negative in nature. Interracial hostility can be read in the tension of bodies, the withdrawal responses, and the glaring expressions of communicators. Actions speak louder than words, and no matter what is said in interracial encounters, no matter what agreements are reached and understandings developed, the truth of the interracial relationship will ultimately be expressed not intellectually but physically. The final and conclusive evidence of positive interracial interaction will be not a figurative ease in racial tension but a literal relaxation of muscle tension, a softening of the brow, a widening of the scowl into a smile. In short, an interracial physical trust must develop, a trust that has been and may still be very long in coming.

Activities

1. In what environments do you normally find yourself when participating in interracial communication? How do you think these environments influence you and your interaction?
2. Choose volunteers from all racial and ethnic groups in the classroom to participate in a nonverbal interracial sociodrama. The participants should present, in front of the class, their impressions of nonverbal behavior of members of other racial groups. The class can then discuss what the nonverbal behavior signifies in terms of the attitudes it communicates and the impact it may have on interracial communication.
3. Observe a series of real-life interracial encounters outside the classroom and describe the nonverbal behavior enacted in such situations. What communicative significance would you attribute to the behavior you have observed? How did the interracial communication participants appear to interpret the nonverbal aspects of their interaction?

NOTES

1. Dean Barnlund, *Interpersonal Communication: Survey and Studies* (Boston: Houghton Mifflin, 1968), p. 511.

2. E. Sapir, "The Unconscious Patterning of Behavior in Society," in E. S. Drummer, *The Unconscious: A Symposium* (New York: Knopf, 1927), p. 137.

3. Jurgen Duesch, "Nonverbal Language and Therapy," *Psychiatry* 18 (1955): 234.

4. Albert Mehrabian, *Silent Messages* (Belmont, Calif.: Wadsworth, 1971), p. 111.

5. Weston Labarre, "The Culture Basis of Emotions and Gestures," *J. Pers.* 16 (1947–1948): 55.

6. Paul F. Secord, "Facial Features and Influence Processes," in Renato Taguiri and Luigi Petrullo, *Person, Perception, and Interpersonal Behavior* (Stanford, Calif.: Stanford University Press, 1958), pp. 300–316.

7. Paul Ekman and Wallace V. Friesen, "Constants Across Cultures in the Face and Emotions," *J. Pers. Soc. Psychol.* 17 (1971): 124–129.

8. E. T. Hall, *The Hidden Dimension* (Garden City, N.Y.: Doubleday, 1966), p. 1.

9. Barnlund, op. cit., p. 54.

10. William Griffith and Russell Veitch, "Hot and Crowded: Influences of Population Density and Temperature on Interpersonal Affective Behavior," *J. Pers. Soc. Psychol.* 17 (1971): 93.

11. Barnlund, op. cit., p. 512.

12. E. Saarinen, *The Search for Form* (New York: Van Nostrand Reinhold, 1948), p. 128.

13. A. H. Maslow and N. L. Mintz, "Effects of Esthetic Surroundings: I. Initial Effects on Three Esthetic Conditions Upon Perceiving Energy and Well-Being in Faces," *J. Psychol.* 41 (1956): 247–254.

14. Norbett L. Mintz, "Effect of Esthetic Surroundings: II. Prolonged and Repeated Experience in Beautiful and Ugly Rooms," *J. Psychol.* 41 (1956): 459–466.

15. Hall, op. cit., p. 1.

16. Robert K. Merton, "The Social Psychology of Housing," *Current Trends in Social Psychology* (Pittsburgh: University of Pittsburgh Press, 1948), pp. 163–217.

17. William Foote Whyte, *Street Corner Society: The Social Structure of an Italian Slum* (Chicago: University of Chicago Press, 1943).

18. Howard M. Rosenfeld, "Effect of an Approval Seeking Induction on Interpersonal Proximity," *Psychol. Rep.* 12 (1965): 120–122.

19. Abraham G. White, "The Patient Sits Down," *Psychosom. Med.* 15 (1953): 256–257.

20. Robert Sommer and Hugo Ross, "Social Interaction in a Geriatrics Ward," *Internat. J. Soc. Psychol.* 4 (1958): 128–133.

21. Ernest Works, "The Prejudice Interaction Hypothesis from the Point of View of the Negro Minority Group," *Amer. J. Sociol.* 67 (1961): 47.

22. Mehrabian, op. cit., p. 78.

23. Robert Sommer, "Studies in Personal Space," *Sociometry* 22 (1959): 247–260.

24. Ibid.

25. Barnlund, op. cit., p. 515.

26. Ibid., p. 516.

27. Gwen Gibson, "Problems Facing Interracial Couples," *Los Angeles Times,* 18 August 1972.

28. Ibid.

29. Mehrabian, op. cit., p. 36.

30. Ibid., p. 37.

31. Ibid., p. 25.

32. Ibid., p. 36.

33. Barnlund, op. cit., p. 519.

34. Lewis R. Aiken, "The Relationship of Dress to Selected Measures of Personality in Undergraduate Women," *J. Soc. Psychol.* 59 (1963): 119–128.

35. Barnlund, op. cit., p. 518.

36. Ibid., p. 519.

37. Mary Shaw Ryan, *Clothing: A Study in Human Behavior* (New York: Holt, Rinehart & Winston, 1966), pp. 37–38.

38. W. J. McKeachie, "Lipstick as a Determiner of First Impressions of Personality: an Experiment for General Psychology," *J. Soc. Psychol.* 36 (1952): 214–244.

39. Monroe Lefkowitz, Robert Blake, and Jane Mouton, "Status Factors in Pedestrian Violation of Traffic Signals," *J. Abnorm. Soc. Psychol.* 36 (1952): 241–244.

40. G. Thornton, "Personality Traits of Persons Seen Briefly," *J. App. Psychol.* 28 (1944): 203–207.

41. Barnlund, op. cit., p. 520.

42. William D. Wells and Bertram Siegal, "Stereotyped Somatypes," *Psychol. Rep.* 8 (1961): 77–78.

43. Paul F. Secord, William Dukes, and William Bevan, "Personalities in Faces, I: An Experiment in Social Perceiving," *Genet. Psychol. Monogr.* 49 (1954): 231–279.

44. Paul F. Secord, William Bevan, and Brenda Katz, "The Negro Stereo-

type and Perceptual Accentuation," *J. Abnorm. Soc. Psychol.* 53 (1956): 78–83.

45. Ibid.

46. Ibid.

47. Malcolm X, *The Autobiography of Malcolm X* (New York: Grove, 1965), pp. 54–55. Reprinted by permission of Grove Press, Inc. Copyright 1965 by Alex Haley and Malcolm X; copyright 1965 by Alex Haley and Betty Shabazz.

48. Ron Tanaka, "I Hate My Wife for Her Flat Yellow Face," in *Roots: An Asian American Reader* ed. Amy Tackiki et al. (Los Angeles: Asian American Studies Center, 1971), p. 46.

49. Ray L. Birdwhistell, "The Kinesic Level in the Investigation of Emotion," in *Expression of the Emotions in Man,* ed. Peter H. Knapp (New York: International Universities, 1963), p. 125.

50. Paul Ekman, "Body Position, Facial Expression, and Verbal Behavior During Interviews," *J. Abnorm. Soc. Psychol.* 68 (1964): 295–301.

51. Paul Ekman, "Differential Communication of Affect by Head and Body Cues," *J. Pers. Soc. Psychol.* 2 (1965): 726–735.

52. William James, "A Study of the Expression of Bodily Posture," *J. Genet. Psychol.* 5 (1932): 405–436.

53. Mehrabian, op. cit., p. 113.

54. Felix Deutsch, "Analysis of Postural Behavior," *The Psychoanalytic Quarterly* 16 (1947): 195–213.

55. Mehrabian, op. cit., p. 115.

56. Edwin Corbin, "Muscle Action as Nonverbal and Preverbal Communication," *Psychoanalytic Quarterly* 31 (1962): 351–363.

57. Allen Raskin, "Observable Signs of Anxiety and Stress During Psychotherapy," *J. Consult. Psychol.* 26 (1962): 389.

58. Maurice Krout, "An Experimental Attempt to Determine the Significance of Unconscious Manual Symbolic Movements," *J. Genet. Psychol.* 51 (1954): 121–152.

59. David Efron, *Gesture and Environment* (New York: King's Crown, 1941), p. 137.

60. Ralph Exline, "Exploration in the Process of Person Perception: Visual Interaction in Relation to Competition, Sex, and Need for Affiliation," *J. Pers.* 31 (1963): 1–20.

61. Ralph Exline, David Gray, and Dorothy Schuette, "Visual Behavior as Affected by Interview Content and the Sex of the Respondent," *J. Pers.* 1 (1965): 201–209.

62. Jay Efran and Andrew Broughton, "Effect of Expectancies for Social

Approval on Visual Behavior," *J. Pers. Soc. Psychol.* 4 (1966): 103–107.

63. N. H. Frijda, "Facial Expressions and Situational Clues," *J. Abnorm. Soc. Psychol.* 57 (1958): 149–154.

64. W. Edgar Vinacke, "The Judgments of Facial Expressions by Three National-Racial Groups," *J. Pers.* 17 (1949): 407–429.

65. Susan Zaidel and Albert Mehrabian, "The Ability to Communicate and Infer Positive and Negative Attitudes Facially and Vocally," *J. Exper. Res. Psychol.* 3 (1969): 233–241.

66. Nico H. Frijda and Els Philipszoon, "Dimensions of Recognition of Expression," *J. Abnorm. Soc. Psychol.* 66 (1963): 45–51.

67. Sandor S. Feldman, *Mannerisms of Speech and Gesture in Everyday Life* (New York: International Universities, 1959), p. 198.

68. Erving Goffman, *The Presentation of Self in Everyday Life* (Garden City, N.Y.: Doubleday, 1959), p. 2.

69. Feldman, op. cit., p. 204.

70. Mark L. Knapp, *Nonverbal Communication in Human Interaction* (New York: Holt, Rinehart & Winston, 1922), p. 7.

71. G. L. Trager, "Paralanguage: A First Approximation," *Studies in Linguistics* 13 (1958): 1–12.

72. G. F. Mahl and G. Shulze, "Psychological Research in the Extra-linguistic Area," in *Approaches to Semantics,* ed. A. T. Sebeok, A. S. Hayes, and M. C. Balston (The Hague: Mouton, 1964).

73. L. S. Haines, "Listener Judgments of Status Cues in Speech," *Quart. J. Speech* 47 (1961): 164–168.

74. Walter H. Wilke and Joseph F. Synder, "Attitudes Toward American Dialects," *J. Soc. Psychol.* 14 (1941): 349–362.

75. Moshe Anisfeld, Norman Bogo, and Wallace Lambert, "Evaluative Reactions to Accented English Speech," *J. Abnorm. Soc. Psychol.* 65 (1962): 223–231.

76. W. E. Lambert, R. C. Hodgson, R. C. Gardner, and S. Fillenbaum, "Evaluative Reactions to Spoken Languages," *J. Abnorm. Soc. Psychol.* 60 (1960): 44–51.

8

An Approach to Teaching
Interracial Communication

The great continuing crisis in race relations makes a course dedicated to the study and improvement of interracial communication mandatory for any discipline concerned with human communication. Such a course, wherever it may be taught, should be designed to promote better interracial understanding and interaction among college students through the study of the theoretical aspects of interracial communication and, most important, through actual student participation in interracial discussion groups.

COURSE OBJECTIVES

General Objectives

The general objectives in a course such as this refer to the learning of broad theoretical concepts. Our first general course objective is: *The student will become familiar with general concepts of communication theory.*

David Berlo[1] presents a model of the communication process which can serve as a superstructure for the organization of class activities. At the same time, such a model provides the student with a solid foundation in the general understanding of the communication process.

According to Berlo's model,[2] the source encodes a message into a symbolic system and transmits it through a channel. The message is then decoded by the receiver, who responds to the decoded message of the source. In responding, the receiver himself becomes a source, and the dynamic process of communication begins again.

All of the attributes of the source and the receiver in the model

Reprinted from Andrea L. Rich and Arthur L. Smith, *The Speech Teacher* 19, no. 2 (March 1970).

will help determine the degree of fidelity with which the message is transmitted and hence will affect greatly the response of the receiver. The code, content, and treatment of the message also will affect the receiver's response.

The goal of effective communication is to have the source's intended message transmitted as accurately as possible so that the receiver responds in the manner desired by the source. When such a response does not occur, a communication breakdown has taken place, which frequently can be diagnosed by reference to the source–receiver, channel, and message attributes presented in the communication model.

The occurrence of such communication breakdowns brings us to our next general objective for the course: *The student will apply his knowledge of the general principles of human communication to the diagnosis of communication problems and communication breakdown.* As we shall see, many of the criteria we employ in student evaluation are based on the developed diagnostic ability of the students.

Specific Objectives

Whereas our general objectives referred to broad theoretical concepts which could apply to any course dealing with human communication, our specific objectives are concerned with aspects of communication theory affecting interracial communication particularly. Using the Berlo model as an organizational framework, we have selected certain parts of the model which seem to apply most directly to interracial interaction problems, and we have framed these areas of study into specific interracial communication objectives.

Our first series of specific course objectives is drawn from the source–receiver attributes of the communication model:

The student will demonstrate an understanding of how congruence or incongruence among communicators in attitudes toward self, the subject matter of the communication, and the recipient of the communication affects the fidelity of interracial communication.

The student will demonstrate an understanding of how congruence or incongruence among communicators in terms of value systems will affect the fidelity of interracial communications.

The student will demonstrate an understanding of how congruence or incongruence among communicators in terms of positions held in the social-cultural system will affect the fidelity of interracial communication.

The student will demonstrate an understanding of how congruence or incongruence of the knowledge level of the subject among communicators will affect the fidelity of interracial communication.

The remainder of our specific course objectives are drawn from the attributes of the message as presented in the communication model:

The student will demonstrate an understanding of how disparity in language codes between communicators affects the fidelity of the message transmission and the effectiveness of interracial communication.

The students will discuss aspects of race relations and interracial interaction problems which concern them as black and white university students.

The students will demonstrate an understanding of how the subtleties of message treatment can project the overt or hidden intents of the source and determine the response of the receiver.

All these objectives will be behaviorized in terms of the class assignments designed to explore each objective and in terms of the evaluative techniques to be employed.

COURSE METHODOLOGY

Teaching Procedures

One method of teaching such a course as this is through the use of an interracial teaching team. Utilizing the benefits to be derived from the use of a team, information can be effectively relayed to the students through the *dialogue-lecture* technique. Here the two instructors discuss topics in a dialogue fashion in front of the class. Though the instructors have certain material they wish to present to the class, they do not employ fully prepared lectures. Instead, they begin to discuss the topics together, inviting the class to join in when appropriate.

We have found such an informal approach beneficial in several respects. First, some of our most insightful and creative ideas are formed in these dialogue-lectures, each of us, at various times, providing stimuli for our partner's creative impulses. Second, we find that conducting these dialogues in front of the class benefits the students. They see firsthand how ideas can be formed through meaningful interaction. They come to understand that our approach is not stagnant, but rather that, in a course of this nature, we thrive on inventive processes and imaginative new ideas. Such an approach seems to stimulate the creative instincts of the class.

A word here might be appropriate as to the benefits to be derived from the use of an interracial teaching team to present a course in interracial communication. While in many speech communication departments the creation of such a team might be impossible because of the limitations imposed by the racial composition of the faculty, when such an interracial team is possible, we strongly urge that it be formed to handle a course such as this. In these sensitive times, if the course is conducted by a black instructor alone, the instructor runs the risk of being accused of black partiality. He might also find it difficult to control the tendency of the classroom to become a black forum. If the class is conducted by a white instructor alone, the instructor most assuredly will be open to criticism on the grounds that he lacks a real understanding of black problems.

A racially mixed team, on the other hand, provides a living example of interracial communication and interracial cooperation. As such, the team tends to set a cooperative atmosphere for the class. Moreover, the combined efforts of an interracial teaching team tend to insure more acute judgments in observing student communication. The strength of a team, as opposed to that of the individual instructor alone, can maintain better class discipline by not allowing unchecked emotionalism to destroy the academic nature of the course.[3]

Apart from the dialogue-lecture approach, we also find the use of *small face-to-face group discussion* to be an effective teaching technique. The class, at various times, is divided into small evenly balanced interracial groups. In these groups, the students discuss various topics dealing with race relations and interracial communication. These discussions provide the students with the opportunity to apply the theoretical concepts of communication he has studied to an actual interracial communication situation.

Closely related to the small group discussion approach is the *class laboratory observation.* Here the discussion groups in the class provide a laboratory for the observation of interracial communication. While one small group is participating in a discussion in front of the class, the remainder of the class observes the discussion group, analyzing and evaluating: (1) the content of the discussion: points of information brought forth regarding interracial communication problems; and (2) the form of the discussion: the application of communication theory principles to the diagnosis of communication breakdown as it occurs in the discussion observed.

We find, then, that the teaching procedures of the dialogue-lecture, the small group discussion, and the class laboratory observation are the most effective means of achieving our objectives in this course.

Selected Class Assignments

The first set of assignments we shall present relates to our source–receiver course objectives. One assignment designed to demonstrate the significance of *value systems* in interracial interaction has been particularly effective. This assignment is divided into three steps. In our first step, the class, with the aid of the instructors, composes a questionnaire designed to reveal the social, moral, political, economic, and educational value systems of the respondents. After completing several outside readings presenting an introduction to value theory, the students design statements created to reveal value differences between the black community and the white community. For example, in the category of political values, the following statement is frequently presented: "The only proper way to effect political change is through the use of established legal channels." It is assumed here that more people in the white community will strongly agree with this statement than in the black community, thus pointing to the possibility that more blacks than whites regard extra-legal means as acceptable in terms of effecting political change. In the economic category, the following kind of statement is sometimes presented: "Anyone who works hard for a living should not be required to support others who fail to provide for themselves and their families." The assumption behind this question is that there will be less hostility expressed toward welfare systems in the black community than in the white community.

Statements such as these serve as hypotheses in terms of the comparative value profiles of blacks and whites. With these statements, black students go into the white community to interview white citizens and white students go into the black community to interview black citizens. In order to insure the student a true interview experience he is required to approach only those people with whom he is not personally acquainted. After the interviews, the class jointly compiles the results they have obtained into a black-white comparative value profile.

In the second step of our value systems assignment, the class members again conduct interviews using the same questionnaire. This time, however, the black students conduct their interviews in the black community and the white students interview in the white community. Again, the class jointly compiles the results into another black-white value profile which they compare with the profile obtained in the first step of the assignment.

We conduct a third step to this assignment if and when a disparity exists between the black and white value profiles and/or a disparity exists between the profiles obtained from steps #1 and #2. This third step consists of a general class discussion. Here members discuss their interview experience, hypothesize as to the results they obtained, and judge which of the profiles compiled are the more valid. That whites may respond differently to an interview conducted by a fellow white than they do to one conducted by a black, and vice versa, frequently provides an interesting topic for discussion and speculation. The students also discuss the relationship between the value disparity between the races and the effectiveness or failure of interracial communication.

Another assignment we employ relates to the importance of *social-cultural positions* to interracial communication. This topic is initially introduced through a dialogue-lecture conducted by our interracial team of instructors. In this dialogue-lecture, we attempt to *stress* that social-cultural position or status occurs intraracially as well as interracially. We want to note that one's social-cultural position is not necessarily synonymous with one's racial identity in the society. Here we emphasize the concept of flexibility and mobility in social status as it affects interracial and intercultural communication.

Finally, we discuss the concept of role playing in our everyday lives and how the roles we assume may change from situation to situation. It is through the use of roles, we suggest, that we are able to predict the communication behavior of those we do not know, and hence, we are able to respond appropriately to a stranger. For example, we expect a priest to behave in a certain manner and are prepared to respond to him in a defined way *before* we ever come to know him as an individual. This process of role playing simplifies our human interaction and the individual decisions we must make in communicating with others. Our position in the social-cultural system can expand or limit the roles we play and our ability to respond appropriately to others occupying a different social-cultural position in our society.

After this introductory dialogue-lecture on social-cultural positions, we again divide the class into small discussion groups concentrating on social-cultural systems as a discussion topic. The students are encouraged to relate the information they have received to their own experience and to express openly their success and failures in role playing and coping with the positions they hold, have held, and hope to hold in our social-cultural system.

We employ a final assignment relating to source–receiver attributes which deals with the effect of one's *attitudes* toward oneself, toward the subject of the communication, and toward the receiver of the communication on the effectiveness of interracial interaction. In this assignment, we ask the students to engage in role reversing. They have thus far in the course participated together in several discussions and have an idea of the attitudes held by their fellow discussants. We now take our small groups and divide them into interracial teams of two, the black participant assuming what he conceives to be his white partner's attitudes toward self, subject, and receiver, and the white partner assuming the attitudes he perceives to be held by his black counterpart. Three sets of partners form a discussion group and discuss a racially oriented topic, reversing roles as they do so.

This experience frequently proves to be extremely enlightening to the students. They find that some of the attitudes they have tried to hide are more transparent than they thought. They discover often that the attitudes they think they project and those they actually project are frequently quite different. Perhaps more than any other assignment, this enables the source of the communication to "get underneath the skin" of the receiver, a receiver who, in this case, happens to be of a different race.

Following the role reversing discussion, the students participate in another discussion, this time assuming their own roles once again. Here they discuss the effects the role reversing had upon them and its implications for interracial communication.

We have found that assignments relating to message attributes are also quite effective in teaching a course in interracial communication. For example, one assignment that seems to be highly regarded by the students deals with the *code* of the message. By code, we mean the particular set of symbols a person uses to express his message. If he speaks in English he has chosen one code; if he speaks in Spanish, he has chosen another. There has been considerable interest lately in the language of the ghetto, some researchers hypothesizing that an actual distinct language code exists.[4]

To check out this theory and its possible effect on interracial communication, we assign our black students the task of going into the ghetto and researching a "black lexicon." Many of our black students are from ghetto areas. This background gives them an expertise which proves invaluable to the class in this area of research. They are asked to develop a brief dictionary of terms they consider to belong to a special and private black code. The black students accomplish this both by calling upon their own personal experience and by frequenting ghetto areas with a new, more acutely sensitive ear for the special meanings given to word symbols by various segments of the black community. In addition, for those non-ghetto blacks who do not know the community language, this task is doubly valuable because it enables them to learn the ghetto vocabulary (the language of intraracial communication) and basic research skills simultaneously. This assignment serves a dual function. First, it provides the class with information that white students alone could not supply. Second, it provides the black students with an assignment which demonstrates the relevance of this course to their personal lives.

When this dictionary is completed, the white students in the class take the terms into the white community, interviewing whites to see if they have any understanding of the black code, and whether their meanings for the terms presented coincide at all with the meanings relayed by the members of the black community. This field work is followed by a series of small group discussions among the class members. The topic of these discussions is: "Does a black lexicon exist; if so, how might it affect interracial communication?"

These are just a few of the many assignments possible in a course of this nature. We feel that the types presented here are particularly beneficial because they are empirical; they are based on the inductive processes of the students themselves. In a course such as this, there can be no dogma. We, as instructors, are discovering and learning, and we feel it is essential that our students discover and learn along with us. Allowed to participate in finding the answers to the many interracial communication problems presented, the students become more personally involved in the course. They take away a greater understanding while they themselves contribute to our knowledge of interracial interaction.

EVALUATION TECHNIQUES

One of our first evaluative procedures is a short essay quiz given very early in the term which is designed to insure an understanding of the general principles of communication theory at the outset of the course. Such an understanding becomes essential to effective participation in later class projects.

The student is also evaluated on the basis of a term project. Such an endeavor is designed to be open-ended in order to encourage students to go into the field, observe interracial communication at work, and write on any aspect of that interaction which interests them. If the student should so choose, he may even conduct a limited experimental project to test some of the hypotheses developed in class. Our emphasis in grading the project is on: (a) the innovation and creativity demonstrated by the student; and (b) the diagnostic skill of the student as exemplified by his ability to discover and attribute causes to communication breakdowns.

The instructors also evaluate the discussion performance of the individual students as they participate in the interracial discussion groups in class. This is viewed together with a judgment of the critical and analytical ability of the students as they observe these in-class discussions. As a discussant, the student is judged on his ability to: (a) avoid causing communication breakdown;[5] (b) institute behavior which will correct a communication breakdown should one occur in the group. As an observer-critic, the student is graded on his ability in a written critique to: (a) perceive communication breakdowns; (b) diagnose the cause of the breakdowns; (c) suggest a course of action which would remedy the problem; (d) pick out any new information presented by the group members, which may provide some enlightenment with regard to interracial communication problems.

The course, as we have presented it here, refers to "interracial communication," communication between blacks and whites. This same course structure can and should be expanded in alternate quarters or semesters to include "intercultural communication," an approach which could encompass the study of communication problems between Asian Americans and the majority society, and between Mexican Americans and the majority society. In this regard, we strongly urge that departments and instructors offering such a course take all steps possible to insure an equal balance among races or cultural groups in each class enrollment. Only in this way can we insure a multicultural approach.

SUMMARY

We have attempted to create a course which is nondogmatic, innovative, and responsive to contemporary needs. We have tried to avoid allowing the class to become steadfast in method or fixed in approach. A course such as this should always be open to revision in order to meet the demands of the time. If an assignment should fail to stimulate student involvement, it should be eliminated in favor of a new approach. Open lines of communication between instructor and student are especially essential in a course of this nature, for here the subject matter is the interracial quality of the class itself. We have learned that student suggestion frequently can provide more insight into interracial communication problems than does much of the scholarly research done in the field.

This course is aimed at combatting the trend toward the increasing polarization between races and cultures in our society. If we achieve only partial success in our small classroom laboratory, we feel our efforts will have been worthwhile.

NOTES

1. David Berlo, *The Process of Communication* (New York: Holt, Rinehart & Winston, 1960), pp. 30–39.
2. Ibid, p. 30. The authors added the term "value system" to two columns in Berlo's model.
3. A warning, perhaps, is necessary here. A course of this nature, if not properly constructed, can easily become a chaotic free-for-all. To avoid this, we feel that a strong teaching team which anchors the course to a solid academic base is necessary.
4. For example, see Joan C. Baratz and Roger W. Shuy, *Teaching Black Children to Read* (Washington: Center for Applied Linguistics, 1969).

5. We do not mean here that discussants must always agree. When an argument occurs, however, our goal is to have such a disagreement based on the issue under discussion and not on a misunderstanding resulting from communication "noise" and interference that can be avoided through an understanding of the communication process.

INDEX